And Then I Smiled:
Reflections on a Life Not Yet Complete

By Dean K Miller

Dean K Miller

MAY 2014

Printed in the United States of America
First Printing, 2014
Hot Chocolate Press

Cover design by: Hot Chocolate Press

ISBN: 978-0-9910626-2-1

www.deankmiller.com

In Memory

Daniel Van Scoy
~
Smiling from above

Contents

Introduction

Every book has a beginning, which is often long before the author starts typing on a keyboard. In keeping with duality and balance, if there is a beginning, then there must be an end. Even though this book has both, neither are the true moments of birth and death, of start and stop, of beginning and end. Rather, what is written here is a collection of moments, neither linear nor random, but recorded moments of now.

You can start on page one, in the middle, or even near the end. It doesn't matter and life certainly won't care. What makes me smile is that throughout our lives, the ups and downs, the lefts and rights, and the would haves, could haves, and should haves, we've managed to arrive here together.

Thanks for making the journey.

~Dean

"Guess why I smile so much?"
"Because it's worth it."

From the Youtube video:
Marcel the Shell with Shoes On Two

Hearts

I rediscovered my writing journey and followed its path. It led to a friend for guidance and advice. She works at a faith-based publishing company and has authored several books and articles. We first met over a decade ago.

We had an initial meeting to discuss my writing. After a few follow-up emails, I was set free like a small bird taking flight into an unknown world. However, after many months on my own, I felt it was time to return to the nest and learn again.

With her typical grace, she found an hour to offer direction to a fledgling writer. We chatted about our lives, our kids, work . . . just catching up. Gradually our discussion turned to writing, both hers and mine. I enjoyed listening as she described her triumphs, as well as her struggles. She explained where she finds inspiration and what gets in her way. She, too, has other writers she turns to for help when she gets stuck. The circle was complete as I returned for help with my work.

As I explained my current project, she listened as if I might be the next Pulitzer Prize-winning author. My questions became her quest to find the best answers. She volunteered to do some research for me, even though I knew her spare time was limited.

We discussed my first piece more fully and she graciously offered to proof read and edit the first draft, as well as providing feedback about any possibility of publishing the final copy.

As we talked she mentioned the exposure she feels when she puts her thoughts to paper, as if she is giving away a piece of her heart. She spoke of the risk and vulnerability that writing produces, and explained how this risk can become its own prison, preventing her from sharing her words, and herself. When I gave her the flash drive that contained my first manuscript, she said I was giving her a piece of my heart.

That was particularly true, given the content of that first draft. However, I no longer fear sharing my heart. I have learned that if you are afraid to share your heart, you become afraid to love and afraid to live. This I will not do.

Instead, I choose to expose my heart to reap the rewards in the smile of a stranger who may read my words and become a friend.

Moments of a Journey

I've journeyed through life, noticing and forgetting, teaching and learning, breathing in and out. I am not lost; so, I cannot be found. A chapter in a just-finished book is titled "Chambered Nautilus." Two days after reading that chapter, I drove past a tree stump carved into an ocean scene, the curved and segmented form of a large, chambered nautilus shell most prominent street side. For me, tranquility always involves water, and often my thoughts return to the ocean.

Tonight's heavy rain will soon change into snow. Already I miss its random beat on my bedroom window. Soon the river will flow wildly, as snowmelt and spring run-off churn through the Big Thompson Canyon. Until the river calms, Leaky Boat Lake is my fishing haven and I return to catching largemouth bass. When I am alone on that small lake, the water seeping through a pin-hole in the boat's bow, I am taken back to when I fished with my youngest daughter in that same leaky boat. She held each fish she caught by its lower lip while I captured the memory on camera. Releasing the fish, she'd laugh when it would flip its tail, splashing cold water on her face. Further back in my memory, I sit with my brother and his son in their boat on a river in Washington.

I watch the interaction of father and son, noticing only subtle differences compared to mine with my three daughters. Our parents taught us well. Still deeper in my memory, I am racing upriver with my father as he deftly guides the wooden craft around logs and gravel bars. We stop to fish, and more often than not, find success. He is a master at the art of fishing and I wonder if I'll ever possess that much knowledge about anything. Beyond that recollection a younger me, wading with my brothers while we fished the small, icy cold rivers fed by the snow fields of Mt. Hood in Oregon. We knew a freedom without bounds—a freedom like one that allows a rock to skip endlessly across a pond.

This evening's moisture began its journey in the Gulf of Mexico. It gave birth to the clouds over the mountains and now cleanses the air, the land, and my thoughts. Should not the rain have the taste of salt, since it was brought from the sea? In the sea and along its shores, I have journeyed far: Hawaii, Oregon, California, Mexico, Florida, New Jersey, Canada, Washington, St. Thomas, St. Lucia. The water was always salty, sometimes calm, sometimes violent, yet always calling to my soul. Riding its waves I have experienced joy as unbinding as is possible, and faced my fears over and over again. Now the river and a small pond hold my humanity in loving care. Their waters will someday reach the sea; in their journey, they will transport a piece of me.

I am alive, and so my passage on this planet is not complete. My wistful memories typed out on keyboard and computer brings "back to now" the moments gone before. They are happening with each step I take.

In an email a friend asked of my memories after sharing one of his own. This is what I'll send to him: "I am lying in the sun amidst a field of green and gold, dreaming of the ocean, knowing I am home . . . and I am smiling."

~ A Second Day of Gray ~

A second day of gray.
More rain; more solitude.
My senses are soaking up
what the droplets offer
nearly as fast as the thirsty ground.

Standing outside in the deluge
it's another chance to look within.
Now the rain; a steady beat on my face–
A welcome respite
a chance to learn, to wash away the fear.
To join the flowers of spring
planting our roots deep
in the softened soil.

That is where we find our strength
the flowers and I;
to express ourselves on the next sunny day,
with confidence, beauty and grace.
Welcoming all who seek
what they think we may hide.
Only to find we truly are
what we appear—
And so much more.

The Apprentice

Time has passed without knowing, creating moments that I may observe. So used to taking the lead, I find myself watching from the shadows. As a back stage apprentice I watch and learn. I am still choosing, but choosing less, and allowing more. I am observing the energy and documenting nothing. Like a leaf upon the river, I am journeying where the flow desires, satisfied with the destination. It is time to accept, not challenge.

There is silence in the winter's night—all sound is muffled by the fallen snow. My breath hangs frozen, shimmering in the reflected light of the moon. I know something is out there, turning thoughts within and I wonder–is *life* ever really the same?

Changing what is perfect. Perfecting what is changed. Creating purity uncommon that releases all which yearns to be free. The surrounding beauty fills the void and winter's cold is shied away. The warmth of the heart stirs again. It is time to move forward, time to change, and time to smile.

Footsteps

Following the footsteps of someone else only leads you to where they went.

You will not find what they found.

It is time to strike out on your own.

The Odyssey of a Monk:
A Step Ahead

Stalled in my writing and seeking inspiration, I tried a new technique called "automatic writing." This entails sitting with pen and blank paper, clearing your mind as best as is possible, and then letting the words come "in." One way to help the process is to ask, either out loud or by writing on paper, a simple question. I wrote across the top of the page; *How can I move forward on this journey?* The following two essays, and the continuing story of the young monk, are the responses to many, such experiments.

*

A child from the Western world traveled with his family to the Far East. After many weeks of boats, trains and horse drawn carts, they reached a small mountain town. Shortly thereafter, an illness plagued the town; the young boy's entire family fell sick and died. He was taken in by the local Buddhist temple, given shelter and care. The young child was allowed to choose his own path, so he began to study their ways.

Time passed and the now teenage monk couldn't escape the sadness he felt when recalling his family's tragedy that had placed him in the temple. Late one night the young monk stole into the room of the temple's holy shrine.

There, in front of the towering gold Buddha statue, he bowed and asked to be set free from his burden.

A gentle voice filled the room.

"A step ahead is all that is needed to not fall behind. Yet a step is nothing more than that. What is the reality you find there? Is it something you've created? Or is it something you are drawn into? Feel the energy of who or what is there. You are never alone. Communicate with those you find along your path. Reaching out is good. Holding within can provide balance. Time has passed and nothing has changed. Looking up brings clouds into view. Looking forward shows where you may go. Look inside to find how to get there. Patience is still, frustration is not. There is not only one, but many for guidance. This has been said before. Numbers do not matter. Your learning is what is important. Time does not determine how far you've come.

"Listen to those around you. There is wisdom to be found. Believe what you see, but know it may hide the truth. Doubt nothing. Make simple connections. One hundred things put together appear as a complex condition. A spider spins one strand at a time, but the finished web looks intricate and complicated. Spin your web in a similar fashion and let it capture your learning. Remember to smile. Do not reach out for your own gratification. Help others first. The hero is not always the obvious choice.

It is often the subtle pieces that complete the puzzle. Open your boundaries, but do not forget what you are protecting inside."

The monk kneeled in front of the statue, placing his hands on his thighs. Looking up in reverence he said, "But it is my feelings inside that have trapped me and are holding me back. I do not know how to release them and cannot move forward."

The source voice of wisdom continued.

"There is much to do on this physical plane. Do not lose your connection there for its gifts are necessary and it is your path to your final destination. How far away is it? How far is the farthest star? Does that not deter you? A simple thought brings it to you in an instant. Follow your intuition and intention. It is all you need to amaze yourself.

"The pending storm is of no concern. A drop of water in a bucket evaporates, even when surrounded by a thousand others. It is no less important because of this action. It is no more important either. Understand and accept that it is, and move forward.

"Do not fret at the emptiness you feel. Accept it and let it go. You cannot be full, if at first you are not empty. The container is not important, the space within is. See it grow and watch it move to places that you have never dreamed. It will be both unreal and the ultimate reality for you. It is but an instant, lasting forever in the infinity of all that is.

"Take time to be that which you are now and see that which you will become. Failing to do so leaves you without a place to grow. If you never set your foot down, you cannot walk forward. Touch that which is around you and know it is real. Then know that the memory is but a dream."

The young monk rose to his feet, bowed to the statue and then slipped away into the darkness, never to be seen at the temple again.

Soul Guidance

Knowing is the way. Guessing leads to confusion and self-doubt. Watch, listen, learn and grow. Sense what you know is the truth. Divine light will lead you. The journey will begin to include others who will receive what you bring. Keep stability in your life. Branch out so the blossoms may grow. Stay rooted in foundation and strength. Honesty and integrity are of utmost importance. Compassion makes many friends. Emotional bonds may be made, but rational thinking and learning will be the way for you.

Separate, but together, the final piece of the puzzle is in your hands and in your heart. Do not doubt what you know. Time is not of the essence. Live in the physical body and see the non-physical through it.

Another shift begins. Another adventure lies ahead. Your steps are sure-of-foot. Balance is the key. Observation is more important now. You will meet others to help you find the way. What happens next is not always up to you, but you will be there at the right place and time. You will act accordingly.

Deep down you have set the path. Many times before you have come here and known—this is my home.

An Unnamed Memory

I read about a beach the other day, unnamed, though I knew which one it was. I set aside the present and spiraled back to moments in my past.

An angry sea lashed against the rocks and cliffs along the shore and the setting sun appeared unsure if it should hasten its descent amidst the fury. Then—a new day, the sea and waves more gentle. Their fury dissipated, they caressed the coves and tidal pools that gave sanctuary to the creatures seeking refuge from yesterday's storm.

Another sunset provided the backdrop as a younger me flew a kite in the offshore breeze. It was a simpler time, with fewer responsibilities. My choice then: to stay or go home. Deciding to stay meant another day to surf, another day to hike the rainforests, or another day to build sandcastles. It was my time to choose. Life held all its promises, but I was happier to push them toward the future.

Maybe I'd head into town, pointing my desires at the bakery that stood amidst the trinket shops along the main thoroughfare. The delicious aromas that wafted down the narrow street drew me in like a moth to a porch light. I fluttered around the display cases, and eyed the treats contained within; various doughnuts, crème filled pastries, luscious cheesecakes, cinnamon rolls and many others.

Finally, to avoid deciding, I chose several different selections, the fresh scent of coffee and baking spices encouraging my purchase. The other patrons smiled and nodded, agreeing with my choices in the large box.

Or maybe, on rare occasion, I'd pick just a single donut and dip it into a steaming mug of hot chocolate as I watched the rain beat against the window. Nearby trees slanted seaward, straining to hold their ground, defying the strong, onshore gusts. The ocean was dark and gray, barely visible through the falling drops.

Braving the storm I wandered onto the sand. At the right spot, I was able to taste both the salty mist from the sea and the fresh water of the rain as they soaked me from head to toe. In the background a lighthouse and fog horn worked in concert, adding a touch of dramatic atmosphere in their routines of guidance for safe passage.

It was there, in the chaos of weather and waves, I felt alive. It was there I found tranquility. It was there I would smile.

Music

Music is the rhythm of my life, and nature's music is a key component. When I escape the noise of society and discover a place of quiet solitude, I find it is easy to listen with my heart. Nature creates its melodies so that we can become part of them.

As long as I can remember, I've appreciated the sounds of nature's hymns, whether it is the call of the sea gulls above the rhythmic crashing of ocean waves, the rustling of dry leaves in autumn or the rolling gurgles of a small stream.

I strain to hear sound in the hush of new fallen snow, and then realize that if I relax, I can hear the quietness of peace within. The symphony of the morning sunrise blends into the deafening silence of the stars at night. All things are in balance, if we let them.

The sound of a crackling campfire takes me back to my childhood. When I close my eyes, I see my family sitting on the sand around a large pot of furiously boiling sea water. My mouth waters as I recall the large, tasty crabs pulled from traps set deep in the salty bay that were cooking in that large pot on the beach. There is laughter in the air and music in our hearts.

Perhaps it is best stated in the closing scene of the movie *August Rush*: "The music is all around us. All we have to do is listen."

Aloha Kauai

It was the evening of our departure from Kauai, Hawaii. For a week we explored and enjoyed the island. Knowing that Kauai contained positive energy, I opened myself each day to the island's mystic offerings. Throughout our visit I discovered bits and pieces of Kauai's magic, yet knew much remained hidden.

We arrived at the airport. While waiting for our flight back to the mainland, I wandered the small terminal. Posted on the walls were photos of Hawaiian dancers, drawings of ancient kings and other cultural images. Below each placard was a short verse printed in the island's native language and also translated to English.

On my fourth trip down the walkways, I stopped at a placard that had previously gone unnoticed. It proved to be the most meaningful moment of my trip. Underneath the photo were the words, *"O KE`OLA NO IA O KIA`I L OKO."*

Translated it means "Look for the life within."

There it was, so simple and eloquent.

The island of Kauai is a tapestry of beauty and grace. When viewed only through our outer senses, it cannot be fully appreciated. Our memories will be like picture postcards, forgotten as soon as they're out of sight.

But if we see the world from the splendor and compassion that lie within ourselves, then the simple moments of joy created in our lives enrich our soul for eternity.

I look forward to another trip to Kauai and the opportunity to allow the island's magic to unfold around me. Until then, I carry that simple message, "Look for the life within." I smile and recall the wonder that is the "Garden Isle."

Solitary by Choice

A sprinkling of truth about the "interconnectedness" of our beings is dawning on me. At some point I'll find the reasons behind it, but for now I am learning that we are all "in this together" even if it seems we stand alone against the world. However, throughout my life (at least the present one that I can recall,) I have relished chances to be solitary by choice.

Long bike rides, crisp morning or warm evening runs and most recently, fly fishing, have all been undertaken without human companionship. But I did not feel alone; somehow I sensed there was more to it. Being alone did not equate to loneliness. I have, admittedly, felt lonely at times. But if I were to scrutinize those moments, I might find that I chose to feel that way, for whatever reasons. And those feelings have always passed.

The human experience is enriched by serving others, by sharing who I am, and by freely offering what I have to give. It is always the others' choice to receive these gifts. I should never be offended by any perceived rejection.

Yet, how do I know who I am, or understand what I really have to offer, if I don't take the time to find out? Basing my self-worth or sense of being on the reactions of others gives away my "power of being."

It reduces my ability to shape the world in the way I see fit.

It is through simple acts of quiet reflection that I am able to begin to understand who I am, what I can become and where I can go. Choosing to go there is an individual decision. Going there alone is a different choice altogether.

I have not found what I am looking for, as I have finally quit looking. Each day I discover more of what I've searched for, without knowing that this is what I would find.

I am nothing that I write, and yet it is everything in me. In this cosmic dance we share the lead. Sometimes I give birth to its wisdom and ways, and other times it leads me down my path, never losing direction and always guiding me home. I will know when I have arrived, for comfort and security will be obvious. I know that I will venture out again into the wild unknown, so that our dance can begin anew . . . and I will smile.

~ Collage ~

I awoke last night,
To the sound of rain.
Like falling pieces of cellophane
That disappear upon the ground.

Fog tiptoes over the valley floor.
A seed takes root and
Begins to grow.

Silence . . .
The children sleep.

The Senses of Life

It is gray, though not necessarily dark. *Foreboding* may be more correct, but being right isn't the concern now. It is the situation. I've traveled here on a road where the toll was paid by decades of choices. There is a smothering feel around me. The darkness is coming, like cascading roll clouds over a mountain top, billowing leeward to windward. I know it is coming. I am powerless to stop it. I'm not sure I even care.

I am alive, because I see it.

There is no need to worry, for light always follows the dark, unless it doesn't. At which point there is no worry, because darkness will rule the landscape. I'm sure it's inside me. But outwardly I feel its clutches. There is no need to scream, for it would be silent. Sound is energy and there is no energy here, except for a laughter that is foul, evil and very real, if I were to believe.

I am alive, because I hear it.

A small flame refuses to be extinguished. It flickers in the soft breeze, casting shadows that grow larger than life as it consumes itself and gains strength. Smoke rises from the valley floor. Creatures flee unsure of what is happening, but know now is the time to run—or die. The earth is barren. Burning hides litter the blackened landscape.

I am alive, because I smell it.

* * *

The season has changed. I saw it coming and still was taken by surprise. The dry, fallen leaves with their caramel-corn crunch signal life has expired. It is not meaningless, it is just—gone. The crisp, vacant air is stirred by the whirling of dead leaves in the autumn wind. Why must they rattle so? Don't they know their time has come . . . and passed?

I am alive, because I feel it.

And now, the turning of a key, the passing of a friend and a voice in the darkness offer hope. Moonlight pierces the clouds; their grip on the night is broken and they recede in fear. The wisp of a memory stirs a beating in my heart. Life courses through my veins. It seems an awakening is on the horizon. Or is it? I bite my tongue and blood oozes into my mouth.

I am alive, because I taste it.

Yes, I am alive.

Raindrops

I stood on the edge of the back patio, the thirsty blades of grass scratching my toes. Overhead, the dark evening clouds provided cooler temperatures and hinted of rain. My gaze turned west, drawn to a small area of concentrated light. The setting sun refused to soften its hues. Isolated through an opening in clouds, its brilliance bathed the foothills. The atmosphere felt hesitant, yet stayed quiet. My thoughts meandered in the solitude. I relished the serenity.

Imperceptibly, the rain began. It stirred my attentiveness as it gathered intensity. Tilting my head back, my face exposed to the rain, I distinguished each drop–some big and some small. There was no other sound, no other sensation. Slowly the rain stopped. I exhaled with the clouds.

In the next moment, a flash of lightning and a sudden downpour. The rain hurtled earthward, loud as a rushing stream as it battered the leaves of the aspen trees. I listened to its fury hitting the pavement.

The water beat against my skin.

Unmeasured time passed.

The rain stopped.

Like the thirsty grass, my soul was refreshed.

My spirit smiled.

The Wall and the Sea

I sat on a log at the beach, spending twenty minutes in quiet contemplation. My thoughts came and went. The gentle crash of the waves, soft sand and warm breeze allowed my mind to drift elsewhere.

I returned to the present moment, unaware of what pulled me back. I watched the waves break along a small river jetty and on the sand in front of me. Across the inlet, the surging ocean ran up against a cement wall, built to keep the higher land and small home from eroding into the sea. With each crashing wave, another tiny piece was worn away. In time, certainly decades, the wall will crumble and the home swallowed by the briny depths.

But the sea was not in a battle with the wall. The waves that appeared to be assaulting it had traveled hundreds of miles, searching their own path of least resistance. Today, that passage ended against the wall. The sea, knowing only its pure self, went as far as it could without fear, without hate, without malice. Upon reaching an abrupt end to its forward journey, it turned back on itself, neither loving nor hating the wall, only knowing its new direction, only knowing itself.

I thought of my present journey in life and wondered what it would be like if I were more like the sea.

If along my path, as I encounter my "walls," (broken down vehicles, a mortgage, kids off to college, frustrations at work,) could I behave in a similar fashion: without fear, without hate, without malice, and without attachment? Would I be able to accept the path of least resistance, not in the manner of giving in, but in the functionality of only doing what needs to be done? (Maybe my assistant soccer coach did have good suggestions.) Could I move on without worry of winning or losing, of poverty or riches, or of acceptance or rejection?

The ocean waves were rejected by the wall, but they did not change themselves. They merely changed the direction in which they were traveling. I smiled at having found a new direction in my life–to proceed without fear. Upon meeting the walls in my life, I will no longer try to break them down. I will simply change my direction without worry of changing myself.

Be

It is easy to forget that everything in life is connected. Reminders are out there, waiting to be discovered. I found one while staining baseboard moldings.

Rubbing the stain into the creases and curves of the wood, the rhythmic motion of spreading and smoothing opened a door of self-reflection. Background music provided a distraction for my thinking mind so that my soul could open to interpretation. Back and forth I worked, gently releasing worries from yesterday, thoughts of today and potential fears of tomorrow. I understood the joy in the creation of a piece of art, be it on canvas, in nature, of stone or wood. The stain blended smoothly where easily absorbed and lingered on places where the wood stubbornly said, "*I will not be changed!*" With patience the stain convinced the grainy wood to become one.

Observing this interplay, I welcomed the thought that "all will be what it must be." And therein lay the beauty and the kinship of the universe. I cannot say why, but I easily accepted the tree farmer's plan to grow the trees so the bark and limbs could be crafted into something. But certainly it was not grown just to be molding. It was grown to be what it was meant to be.

Consider the mill man who cut and shaped the raw wood into this exact design. He knew what the design would look like, for he gave birth to that idea. But he could not have known where the molding would end up, be it business, home or scrap heap.

Or could the stain mixer have envisioned that I would use two different colors to make the blended final color to match my desire? The mixer only knew how to create each stain as it needed to be, so that the final result would be beautiful.

Each musician whose music played in the background could only release the melody as it needed to be, as it was in its completeness, only to become part of a bigger whole.

When I purchased the molding, I certainly did not envision being so moved into acceptance that I would come to know each person's contribution to my efforts, so that I could learn that every life task holds merit and is important not only unto itself, but in becoming part of the entirety.

The Odyssey of a Monk: A Conversation

The young monk had traveled many days and nights, the temple of his boyhood far behind him. As he journeyed he came upon another monk sitting cross-legged on the side of the road. His appearance was of knowledge and wisdom. The young monk kneeled before him, and the elder monk asked,

"What it is that you seek?"

The younger monk said, "Do I possess the key to unlock the door to enlightenment?"

To which the master replied:

"The key is found inside. Is yours hidden, or is it buried under years of ego and doubt? Each day an opportunity presents itself. Release that which is blocking you. There are no locks preventing your quest. There is only your path—which offers a multitude of options. Lay down your burdens. Accept the joy. Let your doubts fly away like so many balloons on a hot summer's day. They grow smaller as they ascend the sky. Soon they are gone, yet you think they are still there. Allow the winds to scatter them like dust. Rejoice in the treasures you find. Know you are a wealthy man, even though you own nothing. Spread your wealth wherever you travel.

"Patience is the key. Jumping too fast won't solve anything and only gives you tired legs.

Be at peace. Be at home. Keep the flames of your heart burning warm and let those who seek it share in its comfort. Answer the door when someone knocks. Who knows what the next friend brings—maybe a new direction?

"As there are fields of grain that wave in the wind, there are those who will help you. Each is waiting his turn and will arrive only when the time is right."

The young monk interrupted the senior monk in front of him.

"I am searching, but can't find them. How will I know if . . . "

The wise monk raised his hand to stop his visitor and continued:

"Stop searching and be. Right here. Right now. Walking a thousand miles is no different than walking a thousand steps. The journey ends when the last step is taken and no sooner. Learning comes at that time. Then it will be time to walk again.

"The frustration of silence is unneeded. Let things be. Let things grow. Watch with quiet eyes. Listen with a clean heart. Be that which is required. All roads lead to the truth which is in your heart and guided by your soul. Focus on 'not-being' what you want and see who you become.

"Gifts arrive, disguised in their wrapping. Only when opened is the true gift found.

"Asking will get you answers. Answers will get you questions. Step out of the circle so you are no longer trapped or isolated within. What do you observe? Is it reality?

"Remember this and you will know."

The young monk reached out, gently took the master's hands into his own and kissed the leathered and wrinkled skin. He then stood, bowed, and resumed his journey. With a second question coming to mind, the monk turned around to again consult the master, only to find the roadside empty and the master gone without a trace.

Reflections from Above

One evening near the end of vacation, I went down to the beach to do my Tai Chi routine. It was close to eight o'clock and the surrounding darkness was topped by patchy clouds. The ocean waves created the perfect rhythm for my practice.

At one point I looked up at the sky. The clouds had parted; above my left shoulder was the Big Dipper. Though hardly a momentous occasion, it was a moment that gently seized my attention. I was over 3,000 miles from home, yet that same stellar formation would be viewable there as well.

Initially, it seemed this might inspire a feeling of insignificance. I am small and the universe is big. What impact can I really have? What I felt instead was not the perception of irrelevance, but of the vastness of the universe around me. As I viewed the astral splendor above, I thought how great it must be to be able to show an identical picture even though I had traveled so far.

I understood then that I was part of this universe not to be trivial, but to be grand as well.

In each moment of life, we choose to be big or small. In that choosing, we create the splendor of our world. Though we did not make the original creation, we are free to "co-create" the next moment of grandeur in the universe around us.

* * *

The Fly That Flew a Thousand Miles

As my flight from Colorado to Oregon descended over the Columbia River, I noticed a fly buzzing about the cabin. The aircraft's flight originated from Chicago, and I wondered if the fly hopped aboard there or in Denver? Either way the fly was now incredibly far from home. But did he know or even care?

It was hard to tell as the fly carried about its business, buzzing around the inside of the airplane, doing whatever it was that a fly likes to do. If that fly decided to exit the aircraft, what would it think? Or do? Upon finding itself in an unknown place, transported far from the comforts of its previous garbage can, would it panic? Or maybe he'd embrace the challenge and set off on a new adventure. The last option would be for the fly to return to his local fly heap and tell all his friends about the strange, new land he had seen so many miles away. If he does, do his fly friends, realizing that he has traveled thousands of miles, start to worship him as the "Lord of the Flies" for his supernatural powers and amazing tales?

We landed. The fly and I deplaned to new experiences, our destinies not so different.

Wisdom from My Soul

At times I feel like the young monk whose story weaves its way through my writing. I found the following words resting in my soul. An evening's walk was taken and the words became clearer.

The time has come to move forward without fear. Know what you perceive to be real. The energy is there, you will receive it. It may take time, but time is not a problem. It's not even real. Mark your days by your learning and growing desire to complete your journey of discovery. Then start a new one, helping others to learn.

A thousand hands reach out to you, not in need (as you fear), but in acceptance, of willingness to guide you to the source. Their love resounds in your heart. You hear it in the music. You see it in nature. You feel it wherever you go. Now is not the time to fret about feeling incomplete. Now is the time to grow.

Those around you will get on board when the ship is ready to sail. No one will be left behind. All will have a life jacket, that being you. But you will not feel burdened. Your load will be light. Your light will guide them home. Listen with open eyes; hear with your inner voice; see by how you are feeling. A smile will brighten someone's day.

The tree takes months to blossom, even longer to bear fruit. Patience will be your strength.

Love will be your path and it will guide you. The moment is now. No one will pass without reason or just cause. Even the blind man knows his way. Your eyes are open. Focus takes time. Be patient. Observe.

Move to where your heart needs to go. There will always be someone with you. Share your heart (and soul) with anyone you choose. It will help them. Know the way is set for you. Take the moment to smile upon yourself; upon your life; upon your growth. Never fear to hold another's hand and know a friend is with you.

I welcomed myself home knowing I was not lost, knowing I would never be alone.

~ Finding One ~

In Solitude, we find Balance.
In Balance, we find Serenity.
In Serenity, we find Ourselves.
In Ourselves, we find our Soul.
In our Soul, we find the Universe.
In the Universe, we find we are One.

The Fire Hopper

It's no secret; my soul rests most easily when I return to the beaches of my youth. It's been a year since I last touched the soft sands of both time and the universe. But our meeting again, like old friends, was comfortable and moving.

The four of us; myself and my wife, our middle daughter and her friend sat by our fire on the beach, its warmth deterring the chill of the starlit sky. One hundred yards away, small waves tumbled in, hushed by the receding tide but still whispering of secrets held under water too long.

We talked about today, wondered about tomorrow and wished the trip didn't have to end. It was the comfort of family and friends drawn together by fire to a time and place of eons long forgotten. How deep in the sand would we have to dig to find ourselves in that earlier time?

Then a wayward traveler stepped into our small circle. He introduced himself as Travis and said he was a "fire-hopper." Travis said he wished to warm his bare feet, the night's cold having nestled into the grains under foot. We welcomed him and shared the usual small talk: "Where are you from? What do you do?" Idle chat flowed easily with this surprise stranger.

A break in the conversation stretched into an awkward silence. Most eyes were cast down to the flame and its phosphorescent coals. I looked up at our guest as he took a few drags from the cigarette he'd lit when he sat down. With each inhale he closed his eyes and drifted somewhere I could not comprehend. I saw the immense pleasure in his gesture and wondered how it moved him so.

A few words followed, then Travis said good-bye, leaving our circle and our fire. He walked 50 yards up the beach to the next flickering, orange-yellow beacon. No one at our site said much about him. He had come and gone without fanfare.

I watched him leave the other fire and walk back in the direction from where he had first come. He stopped, put on a long sleeve shirt and then walked into the darkness and out of sight. A strange encounter, it would seem. I wondered about Travis. What was he really looking for? Should we have inquired of his oceanside quest? Maybe we were too taken aback by his sudden appearance. I pondered these thoughts, curiosity setting in. Had we squandered a chance to learn by not probing about his past? What was his story?

But his intrusion was not wasted. It made me think about my own story. Much had transpired during our few days of travel, a journey that brought me home to the beach. My thoughts drifted, my soul not yet responding. Time had come to take stock of myself.

I discovered pieces of my past, and of myself, that made more sense than much of what I thought was real. For over half a century, I've been writing my story, but I'm only now beginning to understand what is written there, and how I shall write it in the future.

I will never know Travis's story, but that doesn't matter. What matters is he opened up mine.

Seeking

Moving into each day, I often forget the mindfulness needed to bring awareness of each moment into my being. As a result I venture forth, constantly seeking the next thing that creates the peaceful "Ahhh" we all crave, consciously or otherwise. In this wanting and seeking, it is easy to push that which I seek further away. If I find what I am looking for, does that not mean the journey is at end? It seemed like that a week ago, but I've moved past that time by acknowledging what I've learned.

So many seek enlightenment, salvation, redemption, heaven, or whatever they choose to call it. Day after day they struggle through one grievous instant after another. They wonder why they must endure; but endure they do for they (we) seek that final, ultimate goal. However, if they reach their final goal, what then? Have you ever wanted something so bad that you will not be denied, only to find that when you get there, you wonder, "Wow, is that it? What now?" With our eyes so focused on the prize, how much have we missed along the way?

It is said "Life is a journey, not a destination."

But the journey requires focus with every step. Whether good, bad or in between they are but varying degrees of the journey. We are the ones who label them so.

Life doesn't care. It just is, allowing us to make whatever we choose it to be—creating what we choose and then choosing what we believe about that creation.

And in our beliefs we find the reason to smile.

~ In Meditation ~

I have left this place
to journey away from
here and now.
Only to find
I am still here, but
time has not followed.

Like walking into
a different room;
knowing I am
somewhere else,
but in the same location.

Never leaving, I travel
to someplace new.
Senses are heightened,
but none are needed.

All is alive. All is known.
Where vertical and horizontal
never intersect.
Where infinite beauty
is only felt.

I am not alone.
Not in this place.
Feeling home,
away from home.

My heart rests. It's beating
too loud in my chest.
Voices not heard.
Knowledge isn't found
in their words.

I wish to touch
the Creative Divine.
My search begins now, and lasts until
the end of time.

Isle of Sint Marteen—
Christmas Morning

A three-quarter moon floats above the bay, keeping watch as small waves fold themselves along the shoreline. It is Christmas morning, 75 degrees; just a hint of Caribbean breeze sifts into the room.

Last night my wife, three daughters and I watched the Christmas Eve sunset, a blazing orange ornament that slipped into the sea. It belied the feel of season. A fully lit cruise ship crept toward the horizon, with no hope of catching the sun.

I am the first one out of bed, something of an anomaly. Here at the resort, Christmas morning may appear rather normal. The guests and staff might see a jolly old fat guy jog past their rooms and work stations. My twenty-five-minute jaunt takes me around the grounds, then out past the gate and onto the road leading to the port town of Phillipsburg. I take a quick, self-guided tour of the shops and casino of a nearby resort before I head back up the hill and down again to our home for the week.

It is time to settle in to the island's pace of life—Christmas notwithstanding. The American dollar is certainly the local mainstay. I notice an American flag waving in the warm morning breeze next to the St. Martin flag at the entrance to the resort. The Stars and Stripes seem out of place, no disrespect intended.

Maybe the weather and locale lend a *Twilight Zone* feel to Christmas on the island, influencing my thoughts and experiences.

Smitten with floating dreams of freedom, I watch a small schooner work its way out of the bay, toward a destination unknown. It is a way of life that I, too, find necessary. Traveling uncharted waters, I "sail" my way with pen and paper, observing and expressing my thoughts, free from grammar and punctuation rules.

It's easy to reflect on the absurdity of what tourism brings to the island and its people. I know nothing of what has been here before. Nor can I even fathom a guess as to how the islanders' lives would have been if the Europeans hadn't arrived. I find it crazy, seeing a resort employee sweeping sand off the lounge chairs on this Christmas morning. I understand that my being here is part of the reason why he is here, too.

I would've preferred to give him $50 and send him home to his family to spend this holiday, with them. I catch myself and laugh at my self-centered egoism, assuming that I would be "improving" his day by doing so. I have no right to believe I have that much power over his life. Instead, I greet him with kindness, respect, and a Merry Christmas, and then move on my way.

Snow Sweeping Meditation

Arriving home at midnight, I found one inch of fresh snow had blanketed the earth. The temperature was well below freezing. The air was still; not a breath of wind could be felt. The small flakes drifted slowly, as though they wanted to hang in the air forever, knowing the ground would be their final resting place. I put on my hat and gloves and thought about leaving the car running, ensuring warmth upon reentry, but changed my mind without really thinking why. Exiting the car, I retrieved the push broom from the garage.

Starting at the top of the driveway, I brushed the snow toward the sidewalk with ease. It scattered in front of me like powdered sugar. The rhythmic scraping of bristles on concrete was the only sound. A shiver crept up my spine. I stopped sweeping, captured by the silence. I kept my breathing quiet, so as not to disturb the moment, and listened. Only silence, deafening in its completeness.

I began sweeping again, working my way along the sidewalk, past one neighbor's house, and then another. The earlier cold gave way to inner warmth, possibly from the light work I performed; more likely from the surrounding tranquility.

I swept my way from one driveway to the next.

Aware of what I was doing, I was also transfixed by the swishing of the bristles on the pavement. It carried my awareness to a place undefined. I don't recall if the journey led inward or somewhere far away. Standing still, I again listened to my breath. Its steady cadence, like that of my sweeping, cleared my thoughts and defined my being.

I returned to my driveway and removed the light dusting that had since covered my previous effort. I hoped the flakes would end their dance. But it didn't matter. The snow was doing only what it knew, without malice or contempt. It had given itself so that I could be aware of the tranquility of its quiet, allowing me to witness its light in the dark and the beauty of its individuality.

I listened once more and heard nothing.

Peace in silence.

I smiled and began to sweep again.

The Voice at the Tee Box

A sunny morning set the stage for an afternoon round of golf at The Olde Course in Loveland, Colorado. I arrived after the noon hour, warmed up my swing with a small bucket of balls at the range and spent a few minutes on the practice putting green. As a "single" player, I got paired with two other golfers for the day.

We teed off, each of us hitting a good opening shot. As we walked down the first fairway I chatted with one of the other players, he clearly of retirement age. He asked what I did for a living to have a Monday off. I told him that I worked as an air traffic controller. Immediately he asked if I had heard about the plane crash that killed U.S. Open Champion Payne Stewart.

I had not heard any of the reports. My fellow golfer only had a few details, understandable as the crash had only been reported an hour or so previous to our tee time.

We continued on with our round of golf, but the relaxed focus that I normally enjoy had disappeared. I was truly shocked to hear about the death of Payne Stewart. My mind ran a gamut of questions: How could this happen? He had won the U.S. Open. His star was rising again. Why now?

Holes number two and three were played in a blur—bogey, double bogey, with a missed two-foot putt on number three. I couldn't shake the thought of what had happened to the reigning U.S. Open champion.

Our threesome arrived at the fourth tee box and the two others allowed me to hit first, even though I didn't have "honors" (the best score on the previous hole). I balked at their offer, but they thought it might help get my game back on track.

I stood over the ball, my mind working hard to relax, which isn't the best way to guarantee a good shot. A choppy back swing led to another miss hit. My ball flew hard right, struck the base of a tree only 50 yards away and bounced into the rough. Irritated, I sulked off the tee box and slid my driver back into my golf bag with a little extra force.

Enough crappy golf. I was through fighting the round and the awful score I continued to accumulate. I took my scorecard from my back pocket and stuffed it into one of the zippered pockets on my golf bag. If things didn't improve soon, I decided I would leave the course.

I stood behind my bag, out of sight of my partners teeing off. The first gentleman stepped up and readied himself. As he did, I heard a male voice say, "PUT IT BACK."

My playing partners were engaged in the flight of the just hit tee shot. I looked around, saw nobody.

I didn't really expect to see anyone because somehow I knew who the voice was, and that it meant the scorecard. I don't know how, or why, but I did.

I paused, trying to sort this out. Then the voice spoke again.

"IT IS JUST A GAME. PUT IT BACK."

(It was a gentle, yet serious command.)

How did I hear this? More importantly, why did I hear this? Without answers I pulled the scorecard from my bag and put it in my back pocket. I finished out the round, often repeating to myself, "It's just a game," while recording every poorly struck shot.

After we putted out on the 18th green, I shook hands with my playing partners and wrote down my score for the last hole, a double bogey 6. Before walking off the course I looked back up the 18th fairway almost expecting to see Mr. Stewart in his plus fours, knee-high socks and matching Tam O'Shanter. There was no such vision, but somehow I thought I knew who had spoken.

As soon as I got home, I wrote two pages to record my experience. I had never been inclined to record any other strange event in my life, but for some reason I needed to make sure I didn't forget this one.

I still recall the sound of that voice and its powerful expression. I can't prove it was Mr. Stewart's voice, but I know I heard one.

Since then I've never had another experience like that on a golf course.

But I remember his words and believe he is right.

"It is just a game."

The Odyssey of a Monk:
A Return to the Village

The young monk, now several days beyond his meeting of the master alongside the road, arrived at a small village. Upon entering the community, he learned that his family had stayed there before moving to the temple where the illness decimated his family. The village members rejoiced of his return and asked about his voyage. As he recounted his experiences, they listened with respect and reverence of his suffering and his strength.

That evening, after the clans retired to their huts, the monk entered the dwelling of the village shaman. He bowed in greeting and then knelt before the shaman.

"You have returned and yet, still are seeking."

"It is true, master," the young monk began. "Am I awakening on this journey? Looking back I see nothing but foggy memories."

The Shaman replied:

"You see and believe, and still you don't trust. You watch and learn, and still you have doubts. Every day does not have to be a revelation of knowing. What about the moments? What about the flowers along the path? Fix the leak when it is small so the dam will not break. To ignore it creates a flood which cannot be controlled.

"The wisdom you seek is here, and always will be. The path is meant to be followed. The journey not measured in days, but in boundless joy. Look at what you have received. Is that not enough?"

The young monk bowed in respect and said, "It is more than enough, but I want to feel like I am making progress."

The master replied,

"The desire of wanting produces more wanting. The action of receiving produces more receiving. Would joy and happiness within your family not open you to more of the same? You do not create wealth by locking yourself in your hut with all of your possessions. You would only create a jail of stone and grass.

"Continue to be open to others. Let their questions and learning provide you the answers you seek. Peaceful are the fish who ride the currents, trusting the ocean knows where it is taking them; confident they can handle whatever arises on their way. Look at the moment, trust that you know, doubt nothing except all that appears to be real. Only within the confines of your reality does it matter.

"Your world is both big and small. It is ruled by this moment of truth and what that truth brings you. All things are to be released. Nothing is kept forever—not even love. That is meant to be shared with everything, in each moment. This is the only truth you need.

From there you gain access to all that is—coming from the One—the source of which you are a part, but never apart from.

"What if tomorrow never comes? Is today good enough?"

The monk stood, bowed to the shaman, collected his things and walked away into the night.

An Operation

I started to relax as the initial dose of anesthesia took effect. I wanted to shiver in the cold of the operating room, but didn't have the energy to spare. In less than an hour, I would be stitched up, ready to heal, but minus my appendix. Apparently it came without a warranty, and 49 years was all I was going to get out of it.

On the count of three, the surgery team lifted me off the gurney and onto the operating table. The anesthesiologist had given me the rundown on his part of the surgery, but by now I couldn't recite what he had told me. I just trusted that he would do his job correctly, in spite of the fact that my failing appendix interrupted his Christmas Eve plans. I heard him say that he was administering the drugs, but don't recall being asked to count either forward or backward.

I faded to a place where I felt no sensations. All sight, sound and touch were vacant. Then slowly I found myself standing at the edge of an ocean. The beautiful, unnamed beach seemed familiar. The wet sand squished between my toes as the first gentle waves began to lap at my ankles. The water offered neither warmth nor cold, but I enjoyed its soothing, liquid state. I sighed without sound. Each wave circled higher up my legs.

Without force it gradually engulfed my body until it reached above my waist.

I remained transfixed, allowing this altered reality to be real. I did not panic, feel any rush of adrenaline to run to shore, or worry about the rising tide. I stood alone and knew that I need not fear. I was where I should be, trusting the water, trusting my soul.

As the waves reached my shoulders, I started treading water. With a rhythmically smooth effort, I kept myself afloat, relaxed and comforted by the lack of weight upon my body. I did not feel fatigue; instead I felt reassured that the water knew what I needed. Slowly, the current carried me toward the mouth of a river. There, the river entered the ocean peacefully; the salt water welcomed the fresh water, taking care to balance each other's components. Only one remained.

At the river's mouth, I began to swim. Effortless strokes propelled me against the current. I moved upstream, like a fish returning to its ancestral spawning beds. I did not know if this was a passage home. The banks of the river were lined with rocks and trees. A gentle wind rustled the leaves. Onward I swam without worry of time and without worry of having to reach the shore. The river and I would be together until it no longer was to be with me.

The scenery eased from trees to a meadow, the earthen banks covered with vibrant flowers. The river became shallow, then changed into a small stream. I walked along its soft bed. The sun warmed my skin and dried my clothes. It happened in an instant and happened without question.

I strolled across the meadow and up a gentle knoll. Upon reaching the crest, I stood and observed a splendid mountain: tall, not overpowering, but majestic in its beauty.

Standing there I knew I had reached my destination and my origins. Like the river, I began my life in the mountains. My journey will end with a joining of my soul and the sea, taking care to balance our parts until we are one.

Coming out of the anesthesia the first words I heard were from the nurse. As the gentle fog of my journey evaporated I heard her say, "That must have gone well. Look at you smiling."

Caught and Released

Throughout my life, the beaches of Oregon and Washington were the places I'd found the greatest solace. Amidst ambient fog and the cry of a lone gull, the rhythmic crashing of the ocean waves laid my worries to rest. Losing access to those sandy expanses was an accepted consequence of moving to Colorado; however, shortly after our arrival, I found a new place to refresh my spirit: the Big Thompson Canyon. The canyon's namesake river became a favorite destination, where I allowed the world to be as it chose and embraced my spiritual pilgrimage as I learned to fly fish.

On a late autumn afternoon, cold water swirled around my legs as the sun crested the canyon walls, its warmth penetrating my fishing vest. Golden hues filled the narrow panorama before me. Dry leaves rustled on skeletal limbs, their light percussion barely discernible from the river's rumble. With each cast, restless pieces of my life flittered to the surface, drifting downstream to a far off quarter, already forgotten.

Catching two brown trout further expanded my senses. Their energy, transmitted through line and rod, reverberated into my soul. As I released the fish, the frigid water heightened my awareness of my surroundings.

I waded with ease against the slow current, casting toward deeper pools and edges of shallow riffles. In a moment of time I don't remember, my perception changed. Time hung in the still autumn air, refusing to pass. My awareness lacked a sense of body, or even a sense of self. There was nothing to feel, hear, taste or smell. Yet this void contained total peace and a warm sensation, as if I were wrapped in a blanket just pulled from the dryer.

The soft, inner glow coincided with the opening of my spiritual consciousness. My thoughts, unrestrained by knowledge, reached into the infinite expanse. Eternity existed in those precious moments of knowing. My consciousness harmonized with the collective whole. There was no I, as I was totality.

Below, the physical "me" continued to fish, but the detachment from my external self was complete. I simply observed the scene, having released without effort or thought all earthly bonds. A trout surfaced and swallowed the imitation grasshopper. My rod curled into a question mark as the line tightened against the fish's energy. Instantly, I was drawn back to the river. I guided the fish into my net, more from repetition than cognizant thought. Releasing it, I breathed deeply, trying to recapture the fleeting past. With the nexus broken, I simply returned to self, standing in the cold canyon stream.

I eased from the river's current, climbed the rocky bank and sat down.

Eyes closed, I faced the sun, soaking in its radiance, longing to relive the earlier warmth. Overhead, the cry of a solitary hawk reverberated in the canyon. I opened my eyes, watched its shadow stitch along the canyon wall opposite me. The raptor circled once and screeched again. Riding invisible currents, the bird ascended the canyon walls and soared from view, my reverie complete.

I sat motionless, accepting those rarest of moments in my 50 years of life. Though the experience redefined my reality, I also knew there were more secrets out there. Certainly, not all would be found here on this river. Old boundaries were stretched beyond what I had believed possible. The full impact of my experience was yet to be understood. I remained grounded in the earthly realm, knowing I had been touched by the hand of the divine.

Before and After

Recently, I read an article about religion in America. Not surprisingly, over 80 percent of Americans identified themselves as Christians. A large majority of those 80 percent also stated a belief in some kind of afterlife. However, most people simply did not consider the possibility of a previous life. Shouldn't we?

If there is an after, there must be a before. But is this current life the only before that we'll know? Or is this earthly existence already an "after" of something previously forgotten?

Have you ever been somewhere new, but felt it strangely familiar? Do you have artistic or musical talent that is not present in other members of your family? Or possibly you just knew "something" without really knowing why you did? Where do these "things" come from?

If you consider the possibility of a before, can you be sure that the next "after" is really the end? If it is the end, what does this life mean? How does it fit on the path toward enlightenment? Is this really all there is?

So many people seem lost in their day to day living, becoming more of a "human doing" versus a "human being."

We spend countless hours making a living, chasing kids etc., when it might be more beneficial to take some time to rest, relax and reflect on how we are "living."

If you believe *this* is really all there is, then how do you not ask, "What is the point?" Maybe the theme of this life is to figure out what the "point" is? It is something different in the current stream of life for everyone. But each path up the mountain leads to the same summit: life ending in this place and pointing to somewhere new.

Sooner or later we shall arrive.

~ **Dual Rear View Mirrors** ~

You've said before
That, at times, it seems
There are at least,
Two of me.

And looking back
I can somehow see
That maybe
You are right.

And looking back
Is not moving forward.
But just a replay
From where we came.

But looking back
Gives time for growth,
Gives time to learn.
And a chance to look ahead.

Looking at the Past of Me

Much has been said about looking at the past and deciphering its meaning. Does that paint a picture of who I've been, who I am now, or who, I will become? Will the landscape change if we look at it long enough? I recall so much and find so little, only random parts of my life. Is it important that I should carry them with me for so long? What is left if I let them go?

My memories lay scattered like pieces of an unfinished jigsaw puzzle. Some don't seem to fit, no matter which way I turn them. Others create a border around that which I can remember. I am not those memories, but they are a part of me. I try to put them together to make some sense of where I've been. And what do I find? An unassisted triple play in baseball at the age of six, a blue ribbon from a costume parade, and a fish I caught with my grandfather. There's more: an uncle's funeral that corrals a fearful piece of my past, Halloween costumes, sports uniforms, birthday parties with friends. Today, these make me smile. Is it the same smile from my childhood?

Maybe it doesn't matter.

But if I am those assembled pieces, why does the puzzle of my life look so jumbled? Can my soul make sense of the jigsaw moments of my life?

Looking in the mirror, it's easy to see the "finished" puzzle. But if I stare a moment too long, one of the edge pieces slips away and the interlocking ones jumble in my mind. Soon I see that collage of mixed up memories gathered around my feet. Somehow they support me today. Will they tomorrow? What if a new "piece" appears later in the day? Where will it fit? Does an older piece get thrown out, never to be recalled? Am I now missing something that I'll need later? Does this new piece really fit with all the rest?

Questions abound, answers cannot be found.

I think about the past, which seems useless as it is gone. Can I comprehend the truth of what has transpired? And is that truth relevant to now, or just then?

A new bike at Christmas, a football breaking a window, running from the neighbor's yard after retrieving a miss hit whiffle ball, laughing so hard that milk comes out my nose and a long day at the beach riding waves—these are a portion of what I see.

I am different now because of those moments of my history, but shouldn't I feel different too? The mirror reflects how much of this is still with me. Finding more gray hair and a new wrinkle or two, I wonder if they'll be part of the past. Even though I know they already are, I begrudgingly accept them "presently." But what I **feel** is the cold ocean water, the fear of getting in trouble when the window crashed into the bedroom and the disappointment of striking out to end a comeback in a baseball game.

I see myself as I am now but feel the moments as they were then . . . and still are.

But I am different. At least that's what "they" tell me.

I think "they" are wrong. I am the same now as I was then, for all the "thens" were already a "now" waiting for me to be a part of them—like a two-bit actor on a world-renowned stage, playing his part. The understudy patiently waits, knowing his chance may never come. He shrugs his shoulders and accepts his fate.

His time will come if I hesitate.

The Odyssey of a Monk:
A Fathers Voice

Traveling away from the village for seven days, the young monk found himself standing at the edge of a great cliff; a river raged far below. Water crashed in chaotic, white foam against weathered rocks. Distance muted the violence. He heard a familiar voice, infinite in its wisdom, loving in its tone. Bowing his head, he listened.

"You know about the river, its path gently worn into place, moving to the point of least resistance—which is equal to most acceptance. There may be dams built, but they collect the river's potential and then gently release the energy to ease its journey.

"The same is true of your soul. You have ventured far. Or have you? Now, just a moment away from your past—and staring into your future, you know where you must go. Find solitude, yet rejoice in community. Know you are never alone.

"Do not take this voyage lightly, but be light of heart. Strangers will come and you will know them as friends.

"Always travel with a goal in mind and partake in the beauty of creation around you.

"Align your energies in tune with your destiny, and release what you accomplish.

Humility, grace, and compassion were my story. Now, Son, it is yours."

Lifting his head, the young man looked across the canyon. A smile creased his lips. He resumed his journey.

Dreams and Others

Dreams are what we make of them. They can tell us a lot or provide an escape from daily reality.

One night I dreamed I was walking along a familiar stretch of beach. As I continued my stroll, the entire seascape became larger and larger, well beyond what I recognized. Suddenly I jumped into the rushing waves. I swam with their energy, moving toward the shore, then away from it and, finally, parallel to it. I did not panic because I knew if I trusted the current, I would be okay. I never reached the shore, but the dream dissolved without tragic consequences.

The next day as I was reading, I came upon a description of "paramita training," and this paragraph:

"This is the picture I prefer: In the middle of the river, with the shoreline out of view, the raft begins to disintegrate. We find ourselves with absolutely nothing to hold on to. From our conventional standpoint, this is scary and dangerous. However, one small shift of perspective will tell us that having nothing to hold on to is liberating. We could have faith that we won't drown. Holding on to nothing means we can relax with this fluid, dynamic world."

After pondering this reading and thinking about my dream, I realized the message I received is that we should never hold something so tightly in our grasp that we choke it off from its own growth.

Instead, we should hold it gently in our hearts, allowing its growth on its own schedule. Upon letting go we find liberation in that which we've cultivated and set free.

Today Is Eternity

During an afternoon of sorting and cleaning, I stumbled upon several dust-covered VCR tapes. (Remember VCR's?) I knew most of them contained World Cup Soccer matches from 2004, but a couple were unlabeled. I put each tape in the VCR player (yes, we still have two working units) and watched portions of each to make sure I wasn't tossing out a family memory.

One of the tapes contained a program about John Denver. My impression of him from this program differed greatly from the public's perception during his life. I watched for a bit and came upon the following quote from Mr. Denver:

"We learn in the presence of other generations. The old need to teach the young and the young need to teach the old. Although I am no less distressed about the earth's needs than when I was younger, I see more clearly now what I can do about it. And I see that it needs doing as I live my life daily and reverently. This isn't the reverence of 'holier than thou,' it's the reverence that says 'Do thy self no harm as we are all here together.'"

I replayed that particular scene and felt the words resonate in my heart. Over the years I have learned what I can do about "it."

I see the past treasures of youth and now relish the simple joys in life.

I have worked to learn from those around me, both old and young. Many people get caught up in *today's* life, wondering when things might get better, or what they could possibly do to help. Immediately my thoughts turned to the "when" part of the question. My reply is to start today.

As the philosopher Philo said, "Today means boundless and inexhaustible eternity. Months and years and all periods of time are concepts of men, who gauge everything by number; but the true name of eternity is Today."

And what is today? It is the moment of here and now. Today is yesterday's tomorrow and tomorrow's yesterday, as it is for eternity. Starting today, whatever it is you do, you do for all eternity.

When enough of us start today, at this place (here) and at this time (now), the Creator will surely smile, for we are, as Mr. Denver said, "all here together."

Alone in the City

I traveled to a local school for an evening work out. The vacant grass field and running track waited for me. The day was sunny and warm, but as the sun dipped closer to the foothills, the first twinge of autumn nipped at the air.

After 45-minutes of hard training, I plopped down in the center of the field and gazed at the Rocky Mountains looming in the distance. Their presence, shadowed in golden hues of the setting sun, reached to a sky darkened by a dusky blue.

How alone can you be in a city of 68,000 people at 7:30 P.M. on a weekday? Given the right moment, you can be very alone.

The solitude, combined with my exhausted, but satisfied physical state, dissipated my inner noise. Nature's eternal beauty quieted my soul.

Take the moment, savor the peace, relish the splendor and smile.

~ Boxing My Soul ~

She held the golden box
High above for all to see.
Then turned it upside down,
And out fell different parts of me.

As I fluttered
Down to the floor,
The crowd crept closer
Silently awaiting more.

Then violently she shook the box,
Reached in and gave a pull.
No longer could I resist,
Out slipped my inner soul.

The crowd fell silent
As they figured at their best.
Did this inner part really fit
With the pieces lying there at rest?

Yet no one volunteered
To make me whole.
So down she bent,
And scooped me up
Then closed the lid
Upon my soul.

I Don't Know

I sit and I wonder, my feelings on too many tangents. This keeps me grounded with nothing but where I am seated. I will move, but only after my thoughts have decided what to do.

I loathe inactivity, except when I am standing in a crystalline river. Then I am still because the world around me is nearing total synchronicity: the rushing water, the whispering wind, small animals scurrying along the river bank, a hawk soaring overhead, all in ordered fashion.

This is life, not deadlines past due, college tuition, thinking of retirement or the latest rejection letter with the ever polite phrasing of words that scream, "YOUR WORK SUCKS, but thanks anyway." I know, however, that it is someone else whose work sucks. Mine, well, maybe it does too. But I care less about the negativity and move on.

Maybe it's because I'm waiting—waiting for a box with books. Not books I have written, but my books nonetheless because my words are inside. Not many, just one story's worth along with one hundred others.

Acceptance, rejection: it's always the waiting. The clock ticks in the background and I cannot block it out. Same tick, never a tock. (It must have been made in China.)

Someday it will slow down and mark the passage of time in a defeated mode: reckoning the seconds but losing them along the way.

I wonder if those lost seconds still count.

I don't know.

The Grip of Fear

Many live in fear that someone will take away what they perceive to be theirs. An equal number live in fear that no one will give them what they perceive they deserve. The compilation of these fears often divides families, neighbors, cities, states, countries, and continents. Has the heart of mankind been cast into a dungeon so dark that its love seldom reaches the light of day?

No, it is there, waiting for a place to shine.
It is time to break the grip of fear.

I promise, should I find you in a place of need, I will not ask if you are Democrat, Republican, Independent or Ambivalent. I will not ask if you are pro-life or pro-abortion, if you are for gun control or not; or where your ancestors are from. I will simply offer my hand to help lift yourself to where you desire to be and then let go so you move forward on your journey.

And I will smile, thankful for having found a friend.

Elemental Healing

I journeyed to a place where I found a rock, the sun, the wind and the river. It was where I needed to be. They did not invite, nor did they inquire. And they did not turn me away.

On the edge of the river the rock, warmed by the sun and shaped by the wind, offered a place to sit. I accepted, resting my troubles there.

The sun offered brightness when I was feeling darkness. Its light cast my shadow behind me, affirming that my troubles were there as well. Its warmth reached my core. My soul began to see the light beyond.

The wind carried my cries of anguish, fear and frustration down the canyon, until I no longer heard them. Only the sound of the river remained.

The river accepted my tears, blending their salinity with its own snowmelt clarity. Now part of the river, my tears joined that which is forever, that which is always moving and that which is always here.

Whenever I touch the river, I shall touch my tears and remember: I was cleansed by the water and my tears were dried by the wind, that my soul was warmed by the sun and my burdens supported by the rock . . .

. . . and I will know I am home.

~ A Cleansing in Colorado ~

There is a cleansing—
Some might say of evil
in this muddy wash that careened
down the canyon.
A fury of froth carried logs, homes, and cars
down a liquid roadway of death.
Unstoppable; Uncontrollable;
Unbecoming of nature herself.
But—

There is a cleansing—
of which we cannot understand.
The hand of God played against
the hand of man. A futile gesture
to believe "we" can contain the unthinkable.
Now not much is left.
But—

There is a cleansing—
in places once deemed safe.
We were wrong or maybe
ignorant; respectful yet cavalier.
"It couldn't happen again.
At least, not so soon." Scars once healed
torn open anew; painful and deep.
But—

There is a cleansing—
As the sun finally parts
the clouds. Too much rain was days ago
yet still they cried their tears into the river
now swollen and brown. What must we endure
except that which we create in concert
or opposition? Only the earth truly understands and
seems not to care.
But—

There is a cleansing—
of river and sky, of towns
and homes, of life and lives which
we may never comprehend—or
possibly don't want to. Grief,
despair, anger, and loss; possibly without
ever moving beyond.
But—

There is a cleansing—
in anguish through time
that never heals, like a child's tantrum
ignored, returned with vengeance on
anyone nearby. Now passed—
energy exhausted, but for its thunderous,
rolling destruction. Landscapes
forever changed, the shadows of history demolished.
But—

There is a cleansing—
which I hope to never
witness again.

In Balance

Crisp fall air greeted me as I headed out for a morning jog. Whispers of horse-tail clouds softened the sun's energy. The only breeze was the one conjured by my slow, methodical effort. Even at such a pedestrian pace, my eyes watered from the cold. Dry leaves rustled underfoot. In the distant west, the Rocky Mountains shivered in a thin shawl of snow.

Reaching a four-lane street, I paused as traffic prevented my crossing. My attention was drawn down to the curb where a small weight, the kind that is hammered on to a wheel's rim after installation of the tire. Somewhere a wheel was out of balance. A break in traffic beckoned me to cross and I resumed my trek while my mind drifted with thoughts of balance and its importance.

A fly fishing trip with a friend two days ago was balanced by working on the house yesterday. This early run will be balanced by a soak in the hot tub, followed later by a chai latte. An afternoon walk with my wife and our dog would settle out with some quiet time spent writing.

While all of these activities take place in the outside world, it is inside where balance is felt. Doing things just for the sake of doing them won't bring internal balance. Neither will giving an equal amount of attention to every impulse in your life.

Standing fearfully in the middle of life, though certainly steady, only freezes you in place. It is reflection about our actions that provides an indicator to our own balance.

I moved through the remainder of my jaunt, sensing my balance was moving into place. A single, small white feather unexpectedly encountered along my path, was enough to confirm my feelings.

The Heavens seemed to agree.

The Explorer Returns

Last night's fog, which shrouded the street lights, had descended to hug the ground. The sand was damp and cold against the soles of my feet. The distant sound of breaking waves, unseen through the brume, cast an ominous mood. Undaunted, I proceeded toward the ocean. Behind me the hotel was obscured, swallowed by the gray moisture. Moving nearer the salty surf, my footsteps exposed dry sand hidden under the wet, thin-crusted top layer. I walked into the enveloping mist, welcoming the solitude and grateful to be heading home.

Dressed in only shorts and a t-shirt, the cool morning breeze met little resistance. A chilled shiver coursed up my spine. Droplets of moisture collected on the hairs of my arms. The constant crashing of waves grew louder. The scent of oceanic decay filled the heavy air. With a final check from where I'd come, I saw the sun's deep, muzzled glow, its heat unable to penetrate the gray. Continuing on, I reached the hard-packed sand, remnant of the receding tide. My feet sensed another drop in temperature. The sea drew me nearer.

And then I saw her. My pace quickened; the first shallow rush of water, chilled from unfathomable depths, covered my toes. I spiraled back in time, memories washing through me as quickly as the wave receded and then another took its place.

The frigid water wrapped around my shins as I waded deeper. It released its grip and proceeded inland. The brief meeting of old friends complete, we both had more to do. We would meet again.

With gentle relentlessness the waves continued to oppose my direction of travel. The cry of a lone gull, unseen in the thickening fog, cawed a warning; I had ventured far enough. Foaming waves crashed mid-thigh. The morning sky, a pale blue along the horizon, became visible through a small portal in the fog. I looked into forever and the vastness of beyond, seeing every possibility of life. I understood what ancient sailors had felt and possessed the knowledge of their ship's captains: another world was out there, waiting to be discovered.

A second cry from the gull signaled my time to return. I retreated from the sea, taking with me its lessons. Each passing wave guided me inland and then returned to its source, accepting its journey as complete and welcoming its new direction.

I reached the hard-packed sand, a traveler from a distant time and yet, from not so long ago, having discovered a new world inside of me. Turning a final time to the horizon, I watched the fog swallow the small opening of clear sky. My future lay inland, my past safely guarded in the salty depths of the sea.

November Solitude

A thin overcast filtered the morning sun, keeping shadows in the canyon at bay. A fog clouds my mind, remnants of yesterday's five hour rat-race on I-70 over the Rocky Mountains. A full night's sleep at home did little to lessen the highway's jangling of my nerves.

Late enough in the morning to miss the canyon commuters, I relaxed behind the wheel. An occasional drift to the shoulder of the highway kept the Big Thompson River in view. Long overdue, my solitary fishing journey was already paying benefits. I turned off the radio, silence my only companion. As I passed Waltonia Bridge, a voice whispered inside my head: "Pull over. It's time to fish."

Without hesitation, other than checking for traffic, I swung the car around and parked in the gravel. I got out of my car and walked to the edge of the pullout. Below, the river plodded its way around large boulders, much less frantic than during summer flows. The cool morning air heightened my senses; a hawk's screech overhead a welcome greeting. It was time to find myself again.

I couldn't recall the last time I was alone on the river. The deft touch of my Elkhorn 3-weight rod was a simple pleasure and a certain change from the 5-weight rod I had been casting over the last month.

Assuredly, any fish caught today would be snack food for the hefty trout I caught in the private lakes west of Loveland, Colorado.

Three casts. That's it. A new stretch of water christened on my third cast. A small brown brought to net. The icy mountain water stung my hands as I released the fish. Turning upstream I hear voices. It's the laughter of young boys. I am there, in memory, fishing with my brothers. The laughter fades and, again, I am alone.

A second fish, this one a larger rainbow, took the fly and eventually settled into the bottom of my net. I looked up expecting to hear the boyish laughter return, but the only sound was that of the river. It matched the sound of my heart.

Time spiraled past. Whirlpools of memories danced between rocks and along the shore. The last fish I caught came from a pool headed by a rock draped in ice. The frozen water looked more like a freshly washed t-shirt hanging on a summer clothes line than it does a reminder that winter is not far off.

I shook the river from my hands, surprised the drops were not tiny jewels of ice. My fingers were numbed, but my soul was warmed and my life energized in the solitude of the Big Thompson Canyon.

The Odyssey of a Monk:
The Walled City

The monk stood outside the oversized wooden doors, the only entrance into the walled city to which he had traveled. Night fall chilled the air. As he raised his hand to pull the rope and announce his arrival via the attached bell, a thunderous explosion filled the city. Overhead, fireworks lit the sky in sparkles of color. *Yes, it is the New Year,* he thought.

He removed the burlap sack from his back and pulled out his journal that he wrote since leaving the village of his childhood. Over the past year, his entries in the journal were a testament and an acknowledgment of his life's path. Writing only in response to moments of "inspiration," the monk knew that many times his contemplations did not reach the written page. Wisps of thought seemed to be lost.

The monk stepped back from the door, sat down and watched the fireworks. Upon their completion he remained seated, viewing nature's infinite, starry display. His quiet thoughts were interrupted when the city doors opened. Walking out to him was a small man, dressed in the robes of a senior Lama. The elder monk gestured with his hand, implying the wandering monk to stay seated. The Lama sat next to him.

After a minute of silence, the Lama spoke;

"Nothing is without cause, for nothing is ever lost. It exists through all time. Much of what is plotted in your journal was pulled from your past. Reading your notes makes them "present" again, as all things naturally are. Recalling memories, such as when you sat on the precipice and bathed your soul with the warm wind and energy of the earth, is fine. But to seek the re-creation of that specific instant and trying to relive that precise feeling, you are no longer creating "Who you are" or moving toward "Who you want to be." Rather, it is stagnation in the present by looking in the past. Knowing these moments and documenting some of them along the way provide a reminder of the learning you have chosen. But it doesn't define you or your destination. That can only be seized in the speck of time known as now, ever changing, always here."

The Lama paused, his gaze fixed on the wooden doors of the city.

The monk took the moment to speak.

"But if I don't look back and know where I've been, how can be sure I am moving in the right direction?"

The Lama replied:

"In those times of reflection do not question why you encountered them, because you were the one who brought them forth. Often their meaning and lessons are not readily apparent. Their manifestation into reality is a reminder of the Creator's desire to allow you to define your learning.

"So your journey continues. Life will be what it is best: life. What I choose to do with it is up to me. What you choose to do with yours is up to you. Whatever brought you here is in the past. Maybe you'll write or speak about it in the future. Maybe you already have. The decision is made, defining that which makes us smile."

The senior monk stood, brushing the dirt from his robes. Facing the wandering monk, he bowed and then walked back into the walled city, leaving his friend to continue his journey.

~ Echoes ~

A voice echoes
through open chambers.
Distant
in vacant quarters.

Deer nuzzle—
Eskimos in forests.
Passion peaks
but somehow leaks.
Evening suddenly cold.

Footsteps—
moving forward, looking back.
Wondering.
Wondering.

A trail forked.
Now the unchosen path.
Chances taken.
Security shaken.
Time to stand, alone.

Family Currents, Home Waters

The rod arched downward, shaking violently with the strain of a fish struggling to free itself. I grabbed the rod with a quick jerk skyward, setting the hook.

"There's one!" I called out, and realized it had been a long time since I had hooked into a fish this strong. The excitement took the edge off the cold, cloudy July morning.

"I'm never on the lucky side of the boat," lamented Danny, my oldest brother.

The fish darted straight down river. In seconds most of the line zipped off the reel.

"Hey, Dad, it's already down by that other boat," I said, nodding my head toward the aluminum jet-sled 60 yards downstream.

"No, it can't be," he replied.

The steelhead surged out of the water just five yards from their bow, landing with a large splash.

"Okay, I guess you're right. Let's get her."

Keeping constant tension on the fish, I pumped the rod up and down like an oil rig, getting a bit more line back with each cycle. I saw a silver flash in the water as the fish took off on a second run downstream. Again, line screamed off the reel, searing the top layer of skin off my thumb as I pressured the spool.

"Keep the tip up," Dad instructed, even though this wasn't my first steelhead.

I smiled. How many times had I heard those same words when my brothers and I fished with him? Dutifully, I raised the rod tip, unsure if he noticed.

As the fish neared, it made one last spirited swim under the back of the boat and out the other side.

"Watch out for the motor, Deano."

I dipped the rod tip into the water, guiding the line under and away from the motor.

"I've got it clear." My arms tightened from the strain of the fight.

Dad stood ready with the net. With a quick jab, he scooped the gyrating torpedo out of the water and set it on the floorboard.

"Fish in the boat!" I called out. High fives ensued all around.

Hooked on the scale, the steelhead trout weighed just over 11 pounds. It was a beautiful specimen: silver sides with contrasting dark gray hues and spots running the length of her back. Since it was a hatchery fish, we could keep her. Thoughts of fresh steelhead on the grill ran through my mind. My brother broke my trance.

"I told you. I'm never on the good side of the boat."

"Hey, I offered you that spot."

"Yeah, sure, whatever," he said. "Nice fish though. Congrats."

The filtering gray clouds relented to the late morning sun as we headed back to the dock. Just as when we were kids, Dad cleaned and filleted the catch while Danny and I unloaded the boat, carrying rods, tackle and remnants of our morning snacks back to the car. The fillets were packed, ready to freeze for my return to Colorado.

We finished up with lunch at a local burger shack and then headed back to Portland. During the drive I planned the next phase of my return home: a trip to the streams of Mt. Hood.

In those snowmelt tributaries, I spent countless hours of my youth fishing with my brothers. Wading in the cold mountain water, I learned how to "read a river," cast light tackle with a technique similar to fly fishing and how to hook and land a fish. I also developed my love for smaller rivers and streams while stalking the wild trout living in their icy realms.

The following day I drove to Still Creek and into my past. Happiness in those days meant a spinning rod and reel, a package of six pre-tied Eagle Claw hooks, a jar of Patzke salmon eggs, enough gas in the tank and a few dollars for Dairy Queen afterwards. Everything else was a distraction.

I turned onto a single lane road enveloped by evergreens taller than I remembered. Random shafts of sunlight penetrated the forest, creating a kaleidoscope of shadow and light. After a few minutes, I recoiled in my seat.

Several new cabins and small homes tucked amongst the trees imposed their presence and suffocated the freedom that once ruled here. I drove on until I reached a construction road block. Disappointed, I started the slow drive back to the highway. However, I wasn't going to leave without spending time with the creek. I stopped and found a trail leading down to the water.

After a short downhill walk I arrived on the bank of Still Creek. I stood and soaked in the sounds. The stream tumbled under a log jam of six fallen trees, its song in sync with the wind murmuring through the limbs of pine trees. The creek flowed against a rock wall and then turned downstream. I leapt onto a large rock overlooking a deep pool. I sat down and inhaled deeply, the cool air settling in my lungs. I was home.

This river was an integral part of my teenage years. My heart stirred as I recalled fishing with my two brothers just upstream from where I sat. Closing my eyes, I drifted with the sound of the water to a distant memory.

"Danny! Danny, come here, quick. I've got one!" I called across the stream.

"Hang on, bro. Hang on. I've got the net."

I played the wiggling trout on my five-foot spinning rod, the river's current providing more resistance than the fish. Danny scooped up the rainbow and lifted it up for me to see.

Just then middle brother Dave walked around the bend, his rubber hip boots strapped through the belt loops of cutoff jeans.

"You're wasting your time with that little thing. You should've been with me." He carried a fish much larger than mine, his finger holding the large trout through its gills.

"No way, man," I said. "Where'd you get that one?" My bravado was a bit deflated.

"Pulled him out of that riffle you walked past five minutes ago. Can't believe you didn't fish it. But thanks for leaving it open."

We all laughed as I held my fish in front of Dave's much bigger catch.

"Your fish is just a hearty meal for mine," he said.

The laughter faded, swallowed by the sound of the churning stream.

Opening my eyes, I stared into the pool below. The patchwork of stones looked close enough to touch, their red, brown and beige colors distinct in the clear water. Against this montage I caught a glimpse of movement. First one, then another and finally a third fingerling trout swam underneath me. Their tiny tails fluttered in the gentle current. They stared back at me, big eyes dominating their heads. The three of them together, like me and my two brothers. My heart settled into a comfortable rhythm as I recalled a different fishing trip with my brothers to Still Creek.

Danny maneuvered the car down a steep incline to within ten feet of the river. In the starless black of the forest, the headlights lit up the bubbling water creating a disco ball effect on the surrounding trees and rocks. We left the car running so as not to drain the battery.

"You got everything you need?" Danny asked as he shut the door.

"Yeah," Dave said without turning around; he was already making his first cast.

"Hey, wait. My jar of eggs is on the backseat," I said, but the car door closed on my words.

"Get 'em yourself. I'm fishing," Danny said as he took a position downstream from Dave.

I grabbed the door handle and pulled. Nothing happened. I moved to the front door and pulled the handle. That door wouldn't budge either.

"Hey guys, I think we've got a problem," I called above the rumble of the stream.

After 30 minutes and lots of shouting at each other, we fashioned a latch-hook from a stout limb, opened the door and retrieved the keys. The excitement of our night adventure punctured, we fished just a few minutes longer. Dave, as usual, caught the only fish.

The memory floated away on the current below. I left Still Creek and my memories, and drove back to Portland.

I hoped to return to the mountain streams of my youth once more before I flew back to Colorado.

At midafternoon the following day I pulled into my dad's driveway. A lifelong fisherman, he's never cast a fly, but I knew he wouldn't pass up a chance to join me on the river. While I stocked a small cooler with food and drink, he grabbed a pair of old tennis shoes so I could wet-wade without ruining the only pair of shoes I'd brought from Colorado. Driving out to the highway, we passed the site of his childhood home, long since torn down, making way for a car dealership.

"One time, back in '47, your grandfather took me fishing. I must've been about eleven or so. We drove up by Bonneville Dam to a place called Tanner Creek Pool. I took you and your brothers there once or twice. I don't know if you remember or not."

I couldn't recall, but didn't interrupt his tale.

"Your Grandpa and I fished with bright red spinners set above red feathered, 4/0 treble hooks. Those hooks, with the feathers on them, were as big as my hand. I couldn't believe we'd catch fish on something like that. We landed five big Chinooks and saw more than fifty others caught. At least that many shook loose before reaching a net. All day long huge fish jumped out of the water and I heard an endless cry of 'fish on.' At the end of the day, my dad let me carry one of the biggest ones to the car. I could barely keep its tail from dragging on the ground.

My dad just waited for me and laughed that quiet, gentle laugh of his."

As I drove on I glanced at my father and saw a contented smile, one I hadn't seen in a long time. He continued.

"The sad part is, I kept those feathered spinners over forty years, and then they were stolen back in 1990. Most of the other gear taken I could replace, but you just can't find those feathered rigs anymore."

There were other stories too, including their fishing for sturgeon at Onion Rock on the Columbia River.

"Danny, Dave and I used to go there," I said. "One day, I caught two sturgeons. Both were about four feet in length. We were using smelt that were pretty ripe. We heaved those things as far as we could. And remember when you and I went up by Bonneville Dam to fish? On the way home the boat trailer got a flat, so I sat in the boat alongside the freeway to keep it safe, while you drove back to get the tire fixed."

"Oh, yeah, I don't think we'd be doing that today, would we? I'd probably end up in jail for abandonment."

Our memories flowed as easily as the waters we fished. We reached the park's entrance and dad paid the five dollar fee. I drove to the parking lot nearest the best stretch of river, its location easily recalled.

We continued our conversation near the car as I threaded the orange fly line through the guides of my brother's fly rod. For the first time, I realized it was not only old, but also stout—at least a 6-weight. Compared to my favorite 3-weight I use in Colorado, it felt heavy in my hands and I had to work around the reel setup for a left-handed angler.

Over the next hour and a half, Dad and I shared moments of our lives, some never mentioned before. Though we couldn't see the river from the parking lot, we heard its rush over the rocks, but neither of us was in any hurry for me to start fishing. Being there, together, was good enough. The evening breeze carried our laughter, tears and memories back to their beginnings. Eventually, we reached a point in our conversation where what needed to be said had been said. It was time to fish.

After a long hug, we started down the winding path. I remembered my childhood days walking with my father. He carried the fishing rods as we walked through the dew-laden pasture to the Wilson River. The past now present we again made our way to the river. Dad fished here on the Salmon River in his younger days; these currents influenced both of our lives. I didn't want to lose this moment.

At the bridge, I saw the river for the first time in more than 30 years. For all that had changed, I found most everything was still the same. We paused mid-span. I stared upriver. Time slipped away.

Energized and yet calm, I felt a blending of youthful exuberance and life's wisdom settle within me.

"It's good to be back. Thanks for being here with me."

Dad placed his hand on top of mine, which rested on the railing.

"Yes it is. Welcome back, Son."

We crossed the bridge and Dad sat on the hand carved wood bench that overlooked the river. I managed my way down the bank and walked a short distance downstream. The cold water swirled around my ankles and crept toward my knees as I reached midstream. Wet-wading in the summertime is my favorite way to fish—icy water numbing my legs, the scent of pine trees floating on the breeze, hawks screeching above and warming by the campfire in the evening. Fishing like this as a kid meant knowing life at its fullest.

I worked a Royal Adams dry fly trailing a small black ant pattern through the riffles and pools. It took a bit to adjust to the heavy rod, but within 10 casts I landed my first fish: a small, brown trout hungry for the ant. I held my catch above my head in salute.

Dad flashed a big smile and gave a "thumbs up." The master acknowledged his protégé, a father simply loving his son.

Over the next hour I discovered that maybe I had changed with the passage of time.

In the days long since passed, I would rush from riffle to pothole and then to the next riffle, chasing the currents to find fish. However, on this evening I moved in harmony with the river, fishing at a relaxed pace. Maybe it was because Dad was with me, and I wanted the evening to last longer than it could. Or possibly I wanted to relish my return home, knowing I couldn't stay long. But I knew that a part of me would always remain here.

As I fished my way upstream toward the bridge, Dad came down and joined me. I landed a few more trout as dusk settled in, the fingers of sunlight no longer reaching the river. We walked up the bank and headed back to the car.

"If you want, I can carry the rod," he said, holding out his hand.

I smiled. Nothing had changed. I was still that same kid lucky enough to go fishing with his father. I handed him the fly rod.

"Sure, Dad. Thanks."

~ Coming of Age ~

You are no more of an adult today
than you were yesterday.

You are no less a child either.
Remember this and greet each day

with all that you are,
and know that life is ready for your best.

The Fabric of My Memories

With three young girls, laughter, squeals and giggles reverberated off the walls, filling every corner of our home. One of their favorite, and, thankfully, less boisterous activities was playing "hair salon." I would be called for my "appointment" after they'd run out of options on their own flowing braids. Back then I had enough hair to beautify with their plastic barrettes, colorful ribbons and stretchy rubber bands. Sitting patiently, three pairs of small hands worked through my hair. I'd hear a snap, feel a slight tug on my scalp and then snickering behind me.

"Ohhh, that looks so beautiful, doesn't it?" More laughter.

"Yes, it is so much prettier than before."

Clapping and jumping accompanied the giggles.

When my appointment was finished I was handed a mirror. Of course, I conveyed my approval of their work as they pointed out their own contributions.

Through the years, as their hair grew in length, mine crept in the opposite direction. For the girls, a scrunchie, a cloth-covered hair tie, became the rage. Available in all sizes, colors and textures, they pushed the rubber band into obscurity. Hair fashion hit the youth market.

The girls' ensembles were not complete without a matching scrunchie. It didn't take long for the bathroom drawer to overflow with enough of them to stock the local Claire's boutique.

When my daughters started playing team sports, it became necessary to fashion hair ties in colors to match their uniforms. Under the guise of team bonding, pizza parties served as a means to create coordinated hair decorations.

Pinking shears and colored fabric covered the floor. By the end of the evening, shreds of material were everywhere, often accented by pizza sauce or a chocolate milk spill.

By the time my oldest daughter reached nine years of age, she enjoyed watching basketball games on television. As a special treat for her, I acquired two tickets to a Seattle Supersonics basketball game. Our father/daughter outing kicked off with a gourmet meal at McDonald's followed by our arrival at Key Arena shortly before tipoff. During the first half, we enjoyed popcorn (over-salted) and soda (over-sugared and under-carbonated).

My daughter's first NBA game needed a memento, something besides a ticket stub. I suggested we go look for something to take home. She jumped out of her chair and was already skipping up the stairs before I got out of my seat. Out on the concourse we located a souvenir stand and her skipping resumed.

Pom-poms, stuffed animals, mini basketballs and t-shirts hung on metal hooks.

She was undecided until her gaze focused on a scrunchie emblazoned with the Sonics logo. Her finger shot out as if she'd seen an elephant across the room.

"That. I want that. The scrunchie."

I paid for the ridiculously over-priced hair tie without further consideration. Returning to our seats, we enjoyed our food and drink, cheering a rare Sonics win. My "date" fell asleep on the one-hour drive home, her new Sonics scrunchie taken from her hair and moved to her wrist for safekeeping.

Her collection of scrunchies continued to grow, until the fashion changed. Without warning, slimmer, sleeker athletic-style hair bands replaced the scrunchies. Eventually most were sold at garage sales or given away. But not all of them found their way to a new home.

When the time arrived for her to leave for college, I was worried. Foremost, had I done the right things to prepare her for life away from home? Then next, would she eat enough or get enough sleep? All of the things I could no longer control scared me.

On the morning of her departure, with most of her life and its few belongings packed into her car, I picked up the final piece to be loaded—her nightstand. As I carried it down the stairs, the top drawer opened a bit. From the back of the drawer slid the Sonics scrunchie purchased nearly a decade ago. I hadn't known she had kept it and I decided to keep the discovery to myself.

The day was difficult enough. Any new emotions from me would only dampen her excitement.

I maneuvered the nightstand onto the back seat, pulled open the drawer and took one last look at that souvenir scrunchie. Dabbing the tears from my eyes, I closed the car door.

"Looks like you've got everything, at least the important stuff."

"Yeah, I think I've got it," she replied, not knowing how true that was, at least for me. She pulled out of the driveway, starting the next chapter of her life. Knowing that her Sonics scrunchie was going with her made it a little easier to say goodbye.

Adrift to Return

Each day calls to offer its blessings. What determines if it is a day of progress or a day of stagnation? Moving through the day without conscious thought or focus means operating on autopilot. The daily routine becomes redundant action without thought, which prevents forward movement.

It's possible to miss many moments, even though details are absorbed. Awareness of the importance to the matter at hand slips by, unnoticed. Obstructions in life and the body prevent growth. As soon as one component seems to clear, another blockage drops in its place. Like treading water, focus becomes on keeping your head above the surface. The fear of drowning subsides and is replaced by the chance of never reaching the shore.

Too many external activities interfere with the internal self.

Being busy is just that...being busy. Awareness has not left, but has wandered from center.

Outside distractions drain time and energy. Those detours, along with the physical breakdowns, draw attention to areas of the body that need healing. In a highly focused mode, it's possible to vacate awareness of the total self. The soul needs the enrichment of peace and detachment. Otherwise, a journey started with complete attention becomes a pathway of futility.

Learning patience and battling complacency, the view is made from a new perspective.

Effort is required to continue on the path as nothing is automatic. The most important thing is this moment. Like a passing storm, it moves away and is gone. But the learning is available in the next, most important moment in life.

Do not grieve for moments passed. They continue to circulate in the web of the universe, returning to awareness when they choose. A deep breath and a moment's quiet can reclaim that which is misplaced. It is time to smile.

Table Settings of Caribbean Gray

From my patio chair I scanned the bay before me. Low clouds spit enough drizzle to obscure the jutting rocks in gray dreariness. Looking down the beach, solitude would be easily found. A definite change in the tropical weather and possibly more. Did the changing conditions reflect an unseen change in me? I felt the same; though in this morning's prose my handwriting skittered across the page in smaller scribbles. Maybe, like my surroundings, I'd coiled in, snake-like. Was I waiting to strike?

I paused. No need to exert energy, yet. The curtain of fog eased out to sea. It was an odd scene to observe. At the Oregon beaches of my youth, the weather and fog moved inland, delivering its life sustaining water to the interior landscape. Life on this island often proposed an unexpected scenario.

A shift in my personal perspectives is mirrored by the transitional elements. Like the seasons, life fluctuations can be subtle, or as violent as a thunderstorm. If I choose to weather the storm, my mood could reflect the changes brought by the parting clouds and warming sun. Suddenly, the overcast lifted off of the bay. The foreboding sky released its oppressiveness. A sign maybe, that the obscurities in my life could clear out as well.

Pelicans arrived from an unknown hideaway and skimmed the small waves, looking for breakfast.

They climbed steep and then at the apex of their ascent, made a sharp banking turn and plunged toward the water. A violent splash erupted as the birds dove into the depths. Then they returned to the surface and pointed their bills skyward. With ungraceful nods they swallow their meal.

The morning sun crested the small mountain top, scattering the tension of the earlier overcast. I uncoiled my emotions, eased from the chair and bounded across the small stone path to the sandy shore. My feet pressed into the cool, wet grains. A small wave found the courage to venture forth, covering my toes. The wave receded and I was left alone; the sun on my shoulder, a clear blue sky above and an ocean of dreams stretching to the horizon.

A Simple Man

I am a simple man.

I live in a world perceived to be extremely complex. Techno-gadgets allow communications to be made across the globe with the simple push of a button. Wires, electrons, satellites and money make it all happen.

Navigating the daily commute to work, my car contains hundreds of intricate parts functioning millions of times on the 30-minute journey without my interference or knowledge.

But I am a simple man.

The stock market trades itself inside out, and then tumbles. Local school boards fight for money. Growing kids head off to college.

Day after day the world beckons for another decision to be made. Finding the time and energy to meet its demands overcrowds the days on the calendar.

But I am a simple man:

Who enjoys a solitary day at a foggy beach, the heavy mist coating my skin with salty droplets.

I am a simple man:

Who relishes the moments of peace near any lake, river or stream. The water, whether a tranquil pond or roaring rapids has but one purpose: to reach the sea. Everything else is secondary. It will find its way.

I am a simple man:

Who finds his soul refreshed by an afternoon thunderstorm. The heavy rain, brilliant flashes of light and rolling claps of thunder tease my senses to be aware, to come alive.

I am a simple man:

Who will rise to greet the morning sun, until my heart no longer knows the beauty of that which makes me smile.

I am a simple man, and I am alive.

The Odyssey of a Monk:
A Letter to a Friend

After many years of wandering, the young monk, now a grown man had settled in a hamlet nestled in a shallow valley. He sat under a tree to write a letter to his friend. While there he asked, to no one in particular, "What more can I do?" He did not expect an answer, but he listened all the same.

Hearing the birds in the branches overhead and feeling the light breeze brushing his arms and face, he smiled. The man heard a voice, familiar in its tone, but new to him. He liked the voice and listened to its story, writing it down without wondering why.

Standing by a river, all life dwells within. Peace is inside waiting to be released—like the dove from its cage. It is important to smile. Take in the views around you and learn to SEE what others choose to ignore. The ocean will call you home. Be at peace where you are. Follow your heart. Listen with your soul. Believe in your abilities. It is your time to learn and then help others safely reach the light. There are those who will laugh at you. Let them. Laughter is good for the soul.

You possess the truth and will express it to become who you are, which is light and source energy. It is of the creator, the one you hesitate to call God. Call "It" what you choose—it is love and forever shall be.

Walk this path for your place is here among us. The path is wide. Guides will lead you. Love will follow you. Laughter will be your nourishment. Open up to where you are, for that is where you are going. Blessed are those who hear your words. The light will shine over the Earth again and YOU will be giving it life.

The man read the story. It delighted him so much that he decided to make the two-day journey over the mountain pass to share it with his best friend. That night, high in the mountains the man slept. While sleeping he dreamed he met his friend in a beautiful garden. They recalled the wonderful times they shared together. The following morning the man awoke full of love and joy. Anxiously, he set off to meet with his friend.

Arriving at his friend's house, he knocked on the gnarled, wooden door. The door opened and he was greeted by his friend's wife, whose somber appearance gave way to surprise upon seeing him. She asked him to please wait as there was something she needed to retrieve. Upon her return she told the man that her husband died overnight in his sleep. She then handed him an envelope and left him in solitude to read her husband's last written words.

Taking refuge from the midday sun under a large tree in front of the house, the man opened the letter. This is what he read:

Dearest Friend: Standing by a river, all life dwells within. Peace is inside waiting to be released—like the dove from its cage. It is important to smile. Take in the views around you and learn to SEE what others choose to ignore. The ocean will call you home. Be at peace where you are. Follow your heart. Listen with your soul. Believe in your abilities. It is your time to learn and then help others safely reach the light. There are those who will laugh at you. Let them. Laughter is good for the soul.

You possess the truth and will express it to become who you are, which is light and source energy. It is of the creator, the one you hesitate to call God. Call "It" what you choose—it is love and forever shall be. Walk this path for your place is here among us. The path is wide. Guides will lead you. Love will follow you. Laughter will be your nourishment. Open up to where you are, for that is where you are going. Blessed are those who hear your words. The light will shine over the Earth again and YOU will be giving it life.

The man remained under the tree for a long time. Finally, he rose, returned to the house and said goodbye to his friend's wife. As he was leaving, she inquired as to the nature of her deceased husband's note. The man turned, smiled and said, "He said that he loves you and that I should follow my heart."

Then he left, unsure of where he was headed, but knowing his destination.

~ Pathways ~

"When two paths meet and share just a moment of
time—side by side—
that is the time of learning and neither shall be lost."

To Stephen

I began formulating a blog entry, tentatively titled "Perspective." Then two days later I learned that a friend and high school classmate had passed away. So now this piece has become retrospective.

My earliest memory of Stephen was back in fourth or fifth grade. A couple of friends and I had gone over to his house to hang out and play. During the visit he brought out a board game that he created. He rattled through the rules and we began to play. All I remember was that we sat there and let him "help" us through the game. I do not recall who won or lost, and that is not important. What is important and amazing is that he had invented a board game.

Then in sixth grade was a moment that I will never release. It was fall and we were in the process of picking teams for intramural flag football. About three or four selections in, I picked Stephen, knowing he wasn't the most gifted athlete (like we all thought we were), but I knew he wanted to play, so I picked him.

During our first game he presented a set of plays that he diagramed (and I am sure researched) for our team to try.

Unfortunately, at that time I was pretty confident that I knew it all and didn't need any "help" running the team. Perhaps I should have listened because "my" team didn't do well

Who knows, maybe the team may have benefited from Stephen's plays?

And now looking back I see the wonderful lesson that he taught me that day. Nearly 40 years later I realized that I don't have to be in charge of everything. Others can share in the plans of our lives. Now, every time I find myself in that position, I remember Stephen and listen to those around me—me, learning from them.

Since our 30th high school class reunion, Stephen and I exchanged emails on a regular basis. The first email he sent made me chuckle. When I read letters from people, I hear their voices and their individual nuances. But Stephen's emails read so fluently even though he always spoke with a stammer. At first I questioned if the emails were really from him! And then I laughed at myself, at my expectations of his speech patterns to show in his writings.

One of his emails inspired me to write an entry for my blog. I sent him that piece in hopes he would know how much I cherished our correspondence.

The piece I wrote ends with the line, "A friend asked me about some memories, after sharing some of his own, and this is what I will tell him: 'I am lying in the sun amidst a field of green and gold, dreaming of the ocean, knowing that I am home...and I am smiling.'" Stephen was that kind of friend.

Since receiving the news of his death, I reviewed his final email he sent me, just nine days prior to his passing. Though it mentioned his long bout with a cold, there wasn't anything else that I read that raised alarms or worries.

A week passed and then I received an email from the coordinator of our "First Thursdays Group." This group was formed to keep the class of '78 in touch by getting together on the first Thursday of every month. Her email included part of one that Stephen had written to her two months prior to his passing. In his email, Stephen mentioned the reason he "liked coming to First Thursday socials: I've been accepted by all of you." After reading this, I re-read his last email to me, and it was then that I saw something wonderful.

Before we allow ourselves to truly be accepted by others, we must first accept ourselves. I see the hints in his words that he had become more accepting of himself, and was making some new plans for his future.

I also believe that in finally accepting himself, coupled with his feeling of acceptance by the First Thursday Group, his soul reached its point of remembrance, of why "it" had become Stephen. In reaching that moment of discovery and purpose, his soul set itself free of the physical bounds of its earthly presence.

I miss Stephen's emails, but I do not miss him, for I carry these moments with me daily.

And I know that on future trips up the Big Thompson Canyon, where I am most at peace, I will find him there, ready to share the moments that nurture my soul. I will greet him, thank him and we will move forward.

So now, I borrow some words from my favorite book, *Illusions: The Adventures of a Reluctant Messiah,* by Richard Bach: "Don't be dismayed at goodbyes. A farewell is necessary before you can meet again. And meeting again, after moments, or lifetimes, is certain for those who are friends."

Rest in peace, Stephen, if you so choose. But allow me to suggest that you let your soul dance to the outer edges of eternity, to places of boundless beauty and serenity.

Until we meet again, be well, my friend.

Thirty Years

Life interceded and I found myself enjoying lunch with a high school classmate whom I hadn't seen since our graduation 30 years prior. We were good friends in school, but our life paths had taken us in widely different directions. Yet, here we were.

It is always a special occasion to reacquaint oneself with a friend. We chatted a bit. Then he asked something along the lines of, "So what has happened over the past 30 years to land you here in Colorado?"

As one might expect, I ran through the possible list of answers: everything I've done, or everything our family has done, or something less personal and vague, or maybe life-changing turns both good and bad. We carried on our conversation, mentioning highlights here and there. He related a deeply personal moment. I wanted to ask him to expand on his thoughts, but I decided not to inquire. The interceding years advised me to be cautious.

A couple days later, as I replayed the scene in my mind, I realized the only true answer to his question was simply, "choices." Every moment I make a choice: how to think, how to feel, how to act, what to do or whatever else it may be.

When I make those choices on my own, I am in control. I am consciously choosing that which I believe to be the best choice.

If I make those choices based on someone else's words or situations, then I am merely "hopping in their car" and going along for the ride. It's still my choice, but my reality is now based on what someone else chooses.

Yes, maybe I should have answered his question with that one word: "choices." Over and over I thought about this and wondered how someone would react to an answer like that. "So what have you done over the past 30 years?" Quite simply, I've made choices, some good and some bad, depending on your perspective, but choices nonetheless. The result of all those choices has led us to this moment together, despite all the options that have been available to both of us. As such, this meeting is special, just as if we had planned it so many years ago.

I thoroughly enjoyed seeing him again. We shared many memories and many smiles. I wouldn't choose it to happen any other way.

Thank you, my friend.

Journey to a Moment

I stood in a river, its cool water flowing against my legs. Overhead, a turquoise blue sky is swirled with cotton candy clouds. A breeze whispered through the trees lining the shore.

Upstream are three friends fishing, each a silhouette against the final gasp of the evening sun. To their own rhythms they cast, pause and cast again. Drawn together from different realms, we shared the same microcosm of life. Our separate journeys to this moment began lifetimes ago.

I've been fishing all my life. Rivers and streams in the Pacific Northwest, lakes and ponds, too. Though not the sole outdoor activity in my life, fishing was an integral part in the development of my being. In 2000 I picked up a fly rod for the first time. Since then, with fly rod in hand I've found many places to rest my soul and share a smile.

Fishing nearest me was The Fanatic. She's a newcomer to the sport, picking up a fly rod just nine months prior. On her initial trip it took four hours to land her first trout on a fly. I was honored to be there and share the moment. Her quest for fly fishing knowledge, improved techniques and catching fish is surpassed only by the passionate joy and the release of life's complexities she finds on the river.

Upstream from her stood The Fisherman's Daughter. Her personal essay of the same name describes her longing to be a part of her father's fishing world. Her journey to the river this evening was long overdue. I was grateful to witness her return. Seeing her land her first trout and reconnect to a world that in her youth was close and yet so elusive, added a special vibe to the evening. I know she will return again.

At the top of the drift fished The Pilot. He's married to The Fanatic. At first he wasn't sure why fly fishing had taken his wife hostage. But it looked like he was finding his own niche in the river. Often one to venture upstream on his own, I believe he's searching for the freedom and solitude that he finds as he pilots his small airplane across vast stretches of empty sky. At dusk he returned to fish with us and landed the biggest trout of the evening, releasing the fish just before darkness settled.

I gazed upstream one last time, watching them cast to rising fish. The reasons we are here are as different as the places we've left behind. The river understands, accepting us as we are. The cool waters washed away that which needed to go. Although standing in close proximity, we found solitude in this uncertain world.

Life was as it was meant to be, if only for a moment.

~ **The Anniversary** ~

It snowed today–
on our anniversary.
It's the first I can remember.
The snowfall–not
our anniversary.

Which means I've
forgotten the others.
The snowfalls–not
the anniversaries.

Each flake lingers–
unique moments of our past.
Drifting into memories
of You and me together.
Frosting our dreams;
Then melting streamside.
Becoming something new;
Still a part of us.

The river of our lives;
flowing to a destination
we cannot see.
Along the way
new tributaries are formed,
while others run dry.

Someday
we will reach the sea
and dance upon the sand.

Dear Dad

Dear Dad: I remember—

Fishing for crappies on Vancouver Lake with your dad.

My unassisted triple-play in first-grade baseball.

Shooting hoops in the gym with my brothers and you.

Painting the house green.

Buying that weird pickup/van thing, and I sat on the floor when a cop went by because there were four of us on a seat for three.

Spring break vacations at the high school basketball tournament (two trips to McDonald's on Thursday!).

The day the concrete pavement went in for the basketball court in our backyard.

Walking across the Josie Farm and putting the dollar in the can at the gate, so we could access to the river.

Skateboarding down the driveway around cans and buckets.

Playing whiffle ball next door at the Woods' house.

When we went to play my first round of golf at the par 3 course in Vancouver, Washington.

Fishing at the Oregon coast and hooking that big salmon in the first five minutes we were there. We fought it, lost it, and then sat in the pouring rain for another four hours without a single bite.

Camping trips on the John Day River.

Waiting up for you on "budget vote" nights to hear that we'd have Summer Recreation programs again.

Winning second place in the golf tourney at the Lewis River Golf Course with you and my brothers.

Talking with Claxton Welch and laughing when he recalled that you always said, "Don't get your dobber down." (He admitted to me that he never knew what a dobber was, but he never let his get down.)

Striking out a lot in seventh-grade baseball, and deciding that was enough for me.

Fishing on the Lewis River with you and my youngest daughter. She caught two steelhead trout in 15 minutes.

You and I going to Lewis and Clark College to apply for grant money for my first year of college.

Sitting with you in Mile High Stadium when my oldest daughter kicked a 27-yard field goal in the Colorado 4A championship football game.

Our talk along the river at Wildwood, and fly fishing afterwards.

The day I became a father.

Dad, do not fret if one day your memory of our moments begins to fade. I have lived them all, many times over, and know they are the reasons I am the father that I am today.

A Mother's Patience

A mother's patience is one of her most under-appreciated traits. It starts at the moment of her son's conception, as she is the first to know that life has been created inside her. Though her love for the unborn child is strong and the bond of motherhood already formed, she must wait nine months to hold this unique miracle.

She watches as he grows, withstanding sleepless nights of nightmares, his stuffy noses, tantrums and the scrapes and bruises. Someday her son will become aware of the love, the nurturing, and the guiding. And, finally, of the letting go. But she knows it is on his schedule, not hers.

As he spreads his wings and explores the world, the mother continues to wait. Whether it's late-night phone calls, listening to girlfriend troubles, the lack of money or the feeling of not knowing where to go in life, she is there when called upon. Patiently she watches him, knowing in her heart that the choices are his, and sometimes wishing he would choose differently.

But wisdom, learned perhaps from her own mother, has taught her that the journey is not hers to take. Patiently, she watches from afar, understanding that life will teach her son the lesson he needs at the exact moment he needs it.

When he calls to express his frustration, she doesn't try to undo the lesson, but instead helps her son capture the learning.

Then, the moment she has waited for arrives. The son has discovered the true source of his inner self and joyfully returns to her doorstep. With patience she listens to the moments of his life that brought him happiness. Subtly, she encourages his story to unfold, laughing silently at his follies and smiling brightly at his courage to face his fears. He tells her things he has told no one and knows his words are protected and safe.

Though it has taken decades, the bond of mother and son has grown to include a friendship which knows no equal.

Now they walk through life together, knowing their love between them transcends all boundaries. It is everlasting and it makes them smile.

Thank you, Mom, for allowing me to grow into myself, for patiently waiting all of these years for it to happen, and for accepting me each day along my journey. You are the magic behind the story of my life.

The World Within

I came across the following words written by Frederick Buechner in *Telling the Truth*: "You can kiss your family and friends goodbye and put miles between you, but at the same time you carry them with you in your heart, your mind, your stomach, because you do not just live in a world, but a world lives in you."

For many years I lived in a world populated by countless others. It seemed the thing to do. Many came and went, but few left an imprint on my heart and soul. After many years and much learning, I found a world living in me. Now all who come are welcome, just like those who decide to leave as well. Each soul brings a gift, sometimes known, sometimes hidden. Discovering the gift finds a friend. Sharing that gift grows the world within.

Every moment is an opportunity to expand that world. All of us are making up a true story. Limitless possibilities are available. In our choosing, we create our truths. In living those truths, we reveal all that we are.

If we choose to live the next moment as a lie, then that is the truth we create; being true to ourselves should be our highest goal. In doing so we create the self-love necessary to love those around us unconditionally.

Loving those around us, without restriction or judgment, lets us smile at our world within.

Dreams

Close your eyes and see the dream is but a memory wrapped in a smile.

Acknowledgments

First and foremost, thanks to my mother, Jeannine Van Scoy. Without your endearing love, support, and honest feedback, this book would not be a reality.

To my father, Cecil Miller; thanks for taking me fishing, sharing your memories and supporting my work.

I am grateful to author Christine Yount-Jones. Without your encouragement I would have balked at writing from my heart. Thanks to Kerrie Flanagan, owner/director of Northern Colorado Writers, Inc. Your friendship and trust in my writing is valued.

Three cheers to Jennifer Top for your editing and feedback and to Teresa Josef-Franklin for the poetry advice. I am indebted to Sarina Baptista, who introduced me to automatic writing.

To authors Patricia Stoltey for sharing your wisdom, Chuck Barrett for your keen eye, Kym Brunner for your honest feedback, Tim Northburg with formatting help, and Laraine Herring for teaching me how to be fierce in my writing, I offer my gratitude. There are many others who have also helped.

Group hugs to my first assembly of email readers (known as "Miller's Musings,) who received my early essays. I am appreciative of your encouragement and hope you find improvement in my words.

To those whose paths I have crossed, thank you for blessing me with your presence. Even a brief encounter can bring a smile and change someone's life.

Finally, to my wife Laura and our three daughters; thank you for allowing me the time to write and providing a lifetime of smiles. I love all of you more every day.

Information and Links

Quote from "Marcel the Shell with Shoes On Two" used with permission. To view the complete video: http://www.youtube.com/watch?v=Ta9K22D0o5Q

For more information about the music of Kathryn Kaye used in the book trailer, visit: http://kathrynkaye-music.com/

Hot Chocolate Press: www.hotchocolatepress.com

Northern Colorado Writers: www.northerncoloradowriters.com

Kerrie Flanagan: www.KerrieFlanagan.com

Jennifer Top: www.jennifertop.com

Laraine Herring: www.laraineherring.com

Sarina Baptista: www.sarinabaptista.com

Patricia Stoltey: www.patriciastoltey.com

Chuck Barrett: www.chuckbarrettbooks.com

Kym Brunner: www.kymbrunner.com

Teresa Josef-Franklin: www.tjfpoems.blogspot.com

Tim Northburg: www.lifeworkelements.com

About the Author

Dean is a freelance writer and member of Northern Colorado Writers. His work has appeared in Chicken Soup for the Soul: Parenthood, TROUT magazine, Torrid Literature Journal and other literary magazines. His essays won three separate contests at www.midlifecollage.com.

For 26 years, Miller has kept the skies safe as an air traffic controller for the FAA and received the National Air Traffic Controllers Association (NATCA) Northwest Mountain Region 2010 Archie League Safety Award. In his spare time, he enjoys fly fishing and he is an avid supporter and volunteer for the veteran's support group Project Healing Waters Fly Fishing. He lives in Colorado with his wife and their two dogs, Bear and Snickers.

Author's Note

Thank you for reading my book. I ask that you take a few moments to leave an honest review of this book at Amazon.com, Goodreads, B&N, my website, and/or any other venue that accepts book reviews.